ON INDIA

ON INDIA.

BY

MAJOR-GENERAL A. MACLEOD.

GYAN

Published by

Gyan Publishing House
5, Ansari Road
Daryaganj, New Delhi-110002
Phone: 011-47034999, 9811692060
E-mail: books@gyanbooks.com

Distribution Network
gyanbooks.com
India, USA, Canada, UK, Australia, France

ISBN: 978-81-212-7204-9 (PB)
First Published, 1872

2nd Impression 2023

Printed at: Gyan Press, Delhi.

ON INDIA
Author: A. MACLEOD

ON INDIA.

ON INDIA.

BY

MAJOR-GENERAL A MACLEOD.

LONDON

LONGMANS, GREEN, AND CO

1872

CONTENTS

I.

ON THE INDIAN MUTINY

It is a well-known fact in the history of India, that there was current among the natives a superstitious prophecy, that, one hundred years from the battle of Plassy, British rule was to terminate in the East. As a matter of course, enlightened Britons looked upon this prophecy, as they do upon all prophecies of this nature, with such extreme contempt, that to mention it would be derogatory to the dignity of their character. In their legitimate assumption of this high tone of moral character, they forget or are apt to overlook two truths, namely, that superstition is a constitutional element of the human race wherever ignorance prevails, and that there is nothing too sacred for immolation at its dread shrines. A sad, fearful, and never-to-be-forgotten exemplification of these truths has been given us in the late Indian mutiny. And it is not alone that this mutiny shows how deep a hold superstition takes upon the ignorant mind, and how great barbarities infatuated human beings are capable of committing, but it also as strongly shows our own culpability in slighting such a terrible element as superstition, wherever it has unlimited control over the human mind. We should have been on our guard against its explosive and deadly fury.

Previous to the outbreak of the mutiny, we had more need than ever to be prepared for any contingency that might arise, and to be more careful in abstaining from everything that might tend to foment or urge on that dark spirit of revolt which was about to culminate at the expiration of the hundred years, but instead of these precautions, it is well known that, on our part, there was the utmost supineness, and more than ordinary recklessness, in unnecessary tampering with the prejudices and feelings of these deluded natives. That they were deluded, and that this prophecy had a deep root in their minds, can be seen from the following anecdote —A few years previous to the mutiny, Subadar Major Ahmed Khan, my most devoted native friend, earnestly urged me to leave India with my family. I knew well that this advice was not a thing to be laughed at, and consequently I more than once pressed it on the notice of General Cubbon, but he, instead of looking upon it as a thing of any moment, did not hesitate to say that I was a kind of alarmist. But although I knew that there was serious cause for alarm, yet I as well knew that it was not my duty to leave India. The course I adopted was that which I had always followed,—

to do my duty faithfully to the Government, and, paying as much respect as was consistent with duty to the prejudices and feelings of the natives, I used suasive and conciliatory means to dispel their deep-rooted delusions. And, I believe, had these principles been acted upon throughout, we should never have heard of the atrocities that were committed in the year 1857. At the same time, it is my firm conviction that good will be the issue of the mutiny, not only to England, but tenfold more so to India

The *apparent* cause of the mutiny was the introduction of the greased cartridge among the natives. This, as it were, gave them a handle or pretext for revolt without any apparent relation to the prophecy alluded to. But I have no hesitation in saying that the natives looked upon this given handle as a providential arrangement for the accomplishment or fulfilment of the prophecy. And it is a fact not to be altogether overlooked, that, at this very time, when it is more than probable that they desired some pretext for revolt, we, as it were, presented them with what they desired That the Hindoos worshipped bulls and cows, and that the Mahometans held swine as an abomination, were facts as well known to Europeans as to natives of India. And the smallest portions of these animals (of the bull to the Brahmin, and of the swine to the Mahometan) taken within the lips was considered by themselves sufficient to subject them to eternal condemnation, or to be sent to Gehanum. Since such was part of their respective religions, our introduction of greased cartridges at such a time was a grievous oversight That the unfortunate Sepoy did dare disobey the British Government in preference to the violation of his fancied creed is a mournful reflection. But this belief of theirs was not all In all places, and on all occasions, there will be found designing and malevolent beings, fit and ready to concoct schemes of mischief whenever a chance presents itself. To increase the horror and dread of the Sepoy that the greased cartridge would be introduced among the native regiments of India, some designing knaves got up a false and distorted rumour that the English missionaries at Delhi had petitioned the Queen of Britain to give orders for the introduction of this cartridge among the native regiments, saying in that petition that the charm of using fat would have all the natives instantly, and by a supernatural impulse, converted to Christianity! This story was kept as secret as death from the English, but was, I believe, transmitted by living telegraphy with the speed of lightning to every native of India, both Brahmin and Mahometan, who owned British sovereignty. And as another instance of the power of superstition, it was not only that the natives believed that the English missionaries had sent such a petition to the Queen, but all the natives, both educated and illiterate, believed that the English believed in the potency of the charm! As a consequence, this story gave animation to the slumbering spirit of revolt, and tenfold impetus to set the Government at defiance, if it should dare to introduce the greased cartridge among them.

From my intimate knowledge of native character, and of the peculiar views entertained by them about cows and swine, I at once guessed that it was possible for them to conclude that the English had introduced the use of the greased cartridge for a trick or charm to have them converted to Christianity, but I never dreamt of the story of the petition to the Queen, nor of the transmission of secret letters on the subject from Delhi to other parts of India. All this I learned afterwards, as will be explained in the sequel.

Now, it is a well-known fact that orders were given by the British Government to introduce these cartridges among the native regiments of India. When the order was to be carried into execution, about seventy men (Mahometans) of the Bengal Native Cavalry refused at Meerut to use these cartridges, as they believed it was better to refuse to obey any government than go to *Gehanum*. These men were tried, and were condemned to prison and chains; and that very night the mutiny broke out

No one knows what a mighty energy was thus kindled in India by this first step of rebellion or insurrection. No one knows how that mighty energy was kept in check from utterly extinguishing a handful of Britons. Had the southern native regiments followed the example of the north, Britain to-day would not have had an acre of ground in India whereon to set her foot. And I well know that the south, at the time of the mutiny, was in as unstable a state as the north, although somehow providentially it was restrained from acting in co-operation with the north. The same derangement of things, with equally powerful instigations to throw off the English yoke, was in the south that was in the north Historical facts can prove this; and I can prove it in a stronger way than has yet been given to history. There was in all India at the time such a breathless suspense and hesitancy of action, that the miracle is how it was kept in subordination, or was finally determined to take, in the south, that turn which it took. This turn decided the fate of Britain. Numerous historical facts can prove that all India was in a disorganized and unsettled state at the time of the mutiny, and pre-eminently so the defection of the 8th Madras Cavalry, which refused to obey the orders of the British officers who were in command of it. The reasons alleged by the men for this disobedience were that their *batta* was reduced while that of the British officers was increased, and that the pensions of their widows, in the event of their being killed, were to be reduced; but the chief cause of their disobedience was the commission of an error similar in kind, though less in degree, to that which originated the mutiny in Bengal, namely, the non observance of, and trampling upon, native prejudices, inasmuch as the order was given for their march on the day of the native *Kootbah*,[1] or great half-yearly feast. This was the real cause of their dis obedience, and not alone the causes alleged against these men. And I may mention that I warned, as in duty bound, General Cubbon of the danger of this order. A very high caste Brahmin, in one of his letters to me (dated 30th January 1870), says on this subject:—"The circumstance of the Madras 8th Light Cavalry having set out on their march on the very morning of the Moharum Kootba was noticed by all the inhabitants, and is even still remembered It showed great loyalty in the men obeying the order." And let me ask, if Hindoos bear so strongly in remembrance for so many years a slight done to the Mahometan religion, can any Christian of any common sense believe that there is no danger of these two races of the same colour combining to overwhelm the white man, who, in their conviction, has broken faith, in disbanding the *loyal* regiments that saved India? But to return. there was, we

[1] The most sacred day to all true believers in Mahomet, when all go early in the morning to pray at their mosques

repeat, in India, at the time of the outbreak of the mutiny, such a breathless suspense and smothered excitement of inward feeling, among all the natives, as to what they should really do, that no human being can now at this distance of time ever realize the pent-up picture of insecurity to every Briton that was written on every native countenance. The tidal wave of the aroused feelings of a mighty nation hung as it were in the balance, not knowing exactly which way to flow. Whether it should still revert in fidelity to Great Britain, which had been so long its guardian and protector, or break loose with unrestrained fury from that domineering spirit of haughtiness that had so long trampled upon all that was sacred to it, was, at the moment, what no man in India dared with certainty predict. Every step of the British was a step in the dark, and every breath inhaled was a breath of insecurity, for the pent-up and aroused feelings of a nation to which they were but a handful hung in awful obscurity over their heads There is not the slightest exaggeration in this picture; on the contrary, it falls very far short of the reality, and it is not therefore without foundation that I think that there has been one remarkable day in my life.

A day or two *before* the march of the 8th Cavalry, and the receipt of the telegram ordering me with 2000 of my Sillahdar horse to proceed to Mirzapoor—at a time when I told no one all that was told me by the natives of the instability of all our native troops—on the very day of the first publication in our own newspapers of the Cawnpore horrors, I had a memorable meeting with my native officers. At this meeting there was a very full attendance of them; and we had a very touching conversation about the murdering of our women and children. However they might inwardly sympathize with the mutiny as a mutiny, there was exemplified by all at this meeting a spirit of just indignation at, and revulsion from, these enormous atrocities, saying that God could not allow the perpetrators of such deeds to go unpunished. I then introduced the subject of greased cartridges to try them On this occasion, as on all others, this subject was instinctively and instantly shrunk from On seeing this I became excited, and spoke out boldly my bad Hindustani, saying, "I see you believe the Government wishes to convert you by stealth. But the English Government has no such intention; nor was it ever possessed of such an idea And let me tell you, that although it should have such an idea, it has not the power to convert men to Christianity by charms Christianity is not of such a nature as to be affected in any way by what goes into the mouth[1] Simple and true Christianity in its essence is, of all the religions in the world, the only religion which is absolutely free from

[1] The greased cartridge had to be put *into* the mouth, and it was to this that they objected

observances and ceremonies. The essence of Christianity is brotherly love, with an habitual sense of the omnipresence of the Divine Ruler of the universe, both of which necessitate purity of thought, temperance of speech, and rectitude of action, not only for the well-being of our brother men, but for the happiness of individual being. In a word, Christianity is the most profound, yet the most simple, religion in the world I am a Christian because I think no other religion in the world so good. And as it is the desire of a Christian, as well as a Mahometan, to convert men of all classes to his own religion, I would be very glad if all of you became Christians, but if any of you can make me believe, or reasonably show me, that your own Hindoo or Mahometan religion is better than Christianity, I will immediately adopt it."[1] This last remark caused a good deal of laughter and merriment, with not a little seriousness at the same time.

After all had left the meeting, and when I was quite by myself in my own *catcherry*, one of my most intimate native friends, Seyed Fuckroondeen by name,

[1] I need not explain that these were not my exact words, but they form the substance of what I, with the aid of Bustian Arancho, my head *munshee* (interpreter or clerk), said to them on that day He was a native Roman Catholic Christian, and was a man of such truth and honesty that he was universally respected, and his word was implicitly believed by all under me On that distant day, to which my thoughts so often revert, I well remember his usefulness in aiding me to explain the truths of Christianity

returned, carrying in his looks, I must confess, what to me was utterly unreadable. Suspicion, secrecy, and excitement were all depicted in his face; but his object I could not at the moment even dream of. On entering the room, without saying a word, he assured himself that there was no one present but myself, then approaching in the manner of a native to his European officer he let me understand that he wished to converse with me confidentially. He was a fine young man, and the only Mahometan enlisted by me as a Sillahdar, and in my time promoted, through every rank, to that of Regimentdar; but I must candidly say that his appearance and movements on this occasion were more than puzzling However, I signified that he might speak out whatever he had to say. He then assured me that *I* had astonished *him*! Until this day, he said that he and every native believed in the efficacy of the greased cartridge to convert the natives to Christianity, and that they had been introduced for that purpose. "What!" said I, "do all the people believe that greased cartridges were introduced and ordered by Government for the purpose of making all of you Christians?" "Yes," said he, "when I, an educated man, believed this, how can you wonder at every man among us believing in it?" He then said, in the most solemn manner, "If you do not give up my name, I can tell you something." I promised perfect secrecy He then told me that a letter had come from a mosque at Delhi to one at Mysore, saying that the English padrees (missionaries) at Delhi had petitioned the Queen of England, saying, "When the Mahometans conquered India, they converted the people by force, and how many Mahometans are there to-day in India, compared to the handful of Christians, after the lapse of one hundred years' labour among them in endeavouring to convert them to Christianity! We do not wish to employ force, but if your Majesty only ordered the Sepoys to use the same cartridges that are used by the English soldiers, all the Sepoys would soon be converted to Christianity."

This then was the belief of these high-caste natives, and of all natives up till this day, and it is not, therefore, without some degree of satisfaction that I now contemplate that I was the means of dispelling such an unfounded delusion, and of restoring confidence in the good intentions of our Government, and continued fidelity to the cause of England I may mention also that on hearing of the *outbreak* of the mutiny, Subadar Major Ahmed Khan warned me again to leave India immediately with my family, but a few days after this meeting, he returned all full of joy and confidence, presenting me with his son and nephew, and two splendid horses for them, to join my Sillahdar force to go to crush the rebels of the north, and saying that the very women were selling their jewels to provide horses for their sons, and that every one was wild to put down the Bengalees, and that all were for the English, and remarking that never had such a sudden turn in our favour been known before.

I took a written statement of Seyed Fuckroondeen's secret information at once to the Commissioner's house, and read it to him. He was unwell at the time. He asked me to give the name of my informant, but I firmly declined, and on this account he was greatly displeased. Next day he wrote to me for the statement, and I sent it to him Had I then given up the name of my informant, and had the substance of the interview come to the ears of the natives, it might have been death by the natives to this young man, and, in my apprehension, the cause of most serious consequences to Britain. So I felt satisfied (leaving even the matter of honour out of sight, that it would have been wrong to betray any one's trust) that I was doing well to conceal the name of my informant even from the Commissioner.

I may mention by the way that I have in my possession letters from a native Indian friend of the highest caste, one bearing on this interview with Regimentdar Seyed Fuckroondeen, and another on the conduct of the natives during the mutiny. The substance of the former, which is the recollections of Seyed Fuckroondeen on being questioned about the matter by my friend, is just the same as I have related above. But over and above this I could now get in India the whole truth of this timely interview with the native officers, and that of the after interview with Seyed Fuckroondeen, proved by most respectable evidence; and I think that a truth of this nature should not be lost sight of by the Government. *If* a matter of such mighty moment as, perhaps, the preservation of an empire depends upon matters of so trivial a nature as candour in matters of opinion and belief, with a just and fair allowance of consideration and toleration for every reasonable belief, however far from perfection of development, or from being in complexion exactly similar to our own, should we not rather strive to be perfect masters of those occult laws of being that determine the actions of men, than strive to be masters of the actions themselves? It is the far more reasonable way to govern,—to be able to control the motives of men, which determine their actions, than to be able to stem the tide of their actions by brute force. By the former mode we not only gain our end in limiting action, but we at the same time gain that respect and confidence which prevent the possibility in future of undue and unrestrained action, whereas, by the latter, we are only able to conquer but not subdue, and, moreover, open a way for the possibility of revengeful and unrestrained action whenever the first opportunity presents itself. I am perfectly justified, therefore, in saying that I and every one else who made it a rule to govern the native Indian by candour and justice have personally been amply repaid by gratitude and respect, besides the resultant good to the State, in cementing through the individual that bond of union to the State which is its only safety and guarantee of stability And in the very few letters which I have had from India since I left, the only thing that gives me pleasure is that grateful remembrance of theirs of my just toleration of their religion, and of my due but not undignified respect to their prejudices and observances. There was one thing, however, which I could not respect in the character of the native—it is the absolute freedom he has in himself of telling a lie He appears to have not a shadow of the sense of the moral depravity of untruth. For expediency, or to please his European master, he can lie with boundless latitude, and evidently without a single qualm of conscience He does not know, or at least understand, that an English gentleman dreads nothing so much as a lie, and that all *great* Englishmen hold that truth is the noblest feature of manhood.

The truth is, then, we cannot retain our hold of India but by the practice of Christian charity and toleration. A kingdom cannot hold its own internal stability but by such treatment of the mass of its people, and far less can it do so in and with a distant empire that has greater latent capacities than itself. And such is the power of fair and kind treatment over the native of India, that his gratitude has no bounds. In another letter I am styled their "father in Scotland," by a member of a deserving family, to whose deceased father I was simply just while in India. I do not mention this from any motives of vanity, but simply to illustrate two truths the one, the capacity and extent of gratitude which the natives of India possess; and the other, to show the power which each individual of British descent has to attach the individual, through the individual, to the State, and thus secure stability and safety to the Empire as a whole. The safety and stability of a State do not depend upon any direct intercommunion and attachment between its head and each individual member of the community, but on the harmony and humane attachments existing between individuals where there is direct intercommunion, not only among equals, but between superiors and inferiors, between the ruling and the ruled. Each member of a State, from the lowest to the highest, must be in harmony with his immediate surroundings, and that State cannot be safe or in tranquillity where this is not the case; but where this exists, there may be a matchless unity of power in the State as a whole, with the most diverse and discordant elements of thought, belief, and even action itself. There must be no interval of any great extent between individuals who have direct intercommunion with each other. These wide gaps or intervals must be immediately bridged, or certainly there can be neither genuine peace between the individuals themselves, nor security for the perpetuity of the State of which they form integral parts.

It was this want of harmony with his surroundings, and the interval between him and his immediate ruler, that made the native of India mutiny. His ruler would not stoop to enter upon the platform of his prejudices, far less allow the possibility that he himself was possessed of any prejudice, and he had therefore to stoop to the more degrading necessity of having recourse to the edge of the sword to quell that inhuman ferocity of action, which, by the use of a little ingenuity of reason and toleration for difference of belief, might never have happened.

Before the mutiny broke out, of all that was in the mind of the south of India no one exactly knows, nor does any one know all the elements of mischief that were at work to instigate to universal mutiny; but, so far as my experience extended, from the day to which I have already referred, there never were more loyal men to the cause of England than were the men of the south. The 8th Light Madras Cavalry men were no exception to this loyalty. It is only that natives wonder till this day at their extreme loyalty. And I may mention that this opinion of the regiment was entertained at the time, not by natives alone, but also by many Europeans. I believe also that the very atrocities of Nana Sahib helped to save India. It is only now that I can realize what I myself was enabled to accomplish on that day; and that I was enabled to do so, and speak with energy against the mutiny, is owing mainly to the enormities which Nana Sahib had committed. Had the mutiny begun in moderation, I, or any other man, could not have appealed to the universal bonds of brotherhood that unite men to men as such, to prove the justice of having it crushed, but the deeds of Nana Sahib furnished room for such an appeal. The indiscriminate murder and mutilation of helpless women and children was too enormous a thing to be sanctioned by any great number of beings in the form of human.

Having now briefly shown the causes that led to the mutiny, and having shown the nature of those causes that kept the Sepoys of the south from joining with those of the north, I shall try to lay before the reader our real position at present in India as the result of the mutiny. I shall not enter upon the details of the enormities that were committed, nor as to how it was crushed by the stern and retributive hand of Britain, as these are known to every son and daughter of the British Empire.

I will only now repeat the facts, that these deluded natives were put down by stern coercion; that this stern coercion was necessary at the time; and that even that retributive vengeance which extended punishment to the whole for the disaffection of the few, was also justifiable and natural at the time; but I would also bring again before the notice of the reader that it was a preponderance of just and fair treatment that kept the south from mutiny, and that this was the salvation of India; that mastery by coercion is uncertain, and of short duration; and that that dominion alone can be permanent which has its foundation in the reasons of men, by obtaining a complete mastery over the motives that determine their actions, by fair, candid, and wise treatment, which not only guarantees security and strength, but even attachment to the Government. I would also observe that the stringent policy which was adopted and pursued at the time, and which was perhaps justifiable, should now be relaxed; for until this is done, and the wide chasm of mental dissimilarity between two distinct races of men is bridged, our hold of India is insecure, and our position there unsafe

The chasm of mental dissimilarity between us and the natives of India cannot be bridged either by coercive measures, or by any domineering assumptions that our modes of thought are absolutely right, and that theirs are absolutely wrong. We can never convert Hindoos and Mahometans to Christianity in this manner, nor make them think and feel as we do in any degree. The only way in which these desirable changes can be effected is by fair treatment; by reasonable appeals to the radical elements of the understanding, wherein all men are alike, and meet upon a common platform, by toleration and forbearance; and by becoming them, as it were, that they may become us. These are the real roads to victory and to the extension and perpetuation of English dominion in India. By pursuing such a course of policy, we would make India to Britain what Britain is to herself—that each individual is as alive to the honour of the Empire as he is to that of his own.

My final propositions are that the stringent and somewhat exterminating course of policy which was adopted after the suppression of the mutiny, and which may have been justifiable at the time, should now be relaxed, and that a course of policy should be adopted that cannot fail to unite the interests of Britain and India, and make the two empires feel and act as one.

It must be evident to any one acquainted with India that the fidelity of the south was that alone that saved India during the late mutiny. But over and above the patent fact that the south did not join with the insurgents of the north, it must also be told that the British were not more willing and anxious for revenge on the insurgents of the north than were the natives of the south. Under my command there was a loyalty and devotion to the cause of Britain that could not be surpassed by any of British descent. Even family property and jewels were mortgaged to aid in equipments for a march that was to extend over 2000 miles. Many a brave Sepoy of the south laid down his life in crushing the mistaken zeal and fury of his brother in the north, and thousands who had not the opportunity afforded them of evincing such loyalty, were ready to follow their example These facts need no confirmation, and though they should, I have abundant documentary evidence to prove their worth and truth. Notwithstanding this zeal exemplified by the Sepoys of Southern India to suppress the mutiny in the north, it must be well known that "on account of the exigencies of the State," a great number of the regiments of Southern India were disbanded after the suppression of the mutiny

I will not even attempt in thoughts of my own to express the feelings that were then engendered in Southern India by the disbanding of these regiments, but, confining myself to that regiment which was under my *own* command, I beg to lay before the reader their petition to the Queen of England, which says more than a volume of words of mine could ever say. Their petition was never seen by the Queen of England, nor ought it to have been addressed to her;

and therefore it was at the time set aside, as it was not got up in due form to the Secretary for India, to whom such a petition should have been presented. As I was made custodier of their petition I promised not to forget them, and I now fulfil my promise in presenting it to the public, this being all that I directly can do. It is now upwards of ten years since their petition was written. I could do nothing for them at the time; but now, at this distance of time, when both Britain and India have recovered their reason from the fearful and unparalleled excitement into which they were then thrown, I trust my efforts in a humane cause and for the lasting good of India and Britain shall not be altogether without success. The following is a literal translation of the petition, prepared by the regimental interpreter, Captain Mulcaster, and it was written and got up by a Havildar, with help from all the native officers of the regiment, with my permission and General (Sir Augustus) Spenser's sanction, and positively without any European assistance.

PETITION.

"*To Her Most Gracious Majesty Victoria, Queen of Great Britain, Ireland, and of India*

"BANGALORE, 1st *December* 1860

"In consequence of the orders of Her Majesty's Home Government, published in Madras General

Orders of the 26th October 1860, disbanding the 6th Madras Light Cavalry, the loyal and faithful native officers, non-commissioned officers, and Sepoys of the 6th Regiment Light Cavalry, humbly venture to represent to Her Most Gracious Majesty Victoria, Queen of Great Britain, Ireland, and of India, that we, Her Majesty's humble servants, have, for the last fifty-nine years, since 1799 up till this date, been her devoted and loyal subjects and soldiers, have established the name and upheld the number of the regiment, and protected the regimental standards, and have fought in many battle-fields as Her Majesty's most loyal and faithful soldiers. In the year 1816, Her Majesty's humble petitioners performed many long marches, and fought valiantly and loyally at the battle of Nagpore. Subsequently, from the year 1840 till 1843, Her Majesty's humble petitioners were present at many engagements in the field in Bundelcund and on the banks of the river Nerbudda, under the command of Brigadiers Williams and Watson, viz., at Harapoor, Simerrali, Nancote, and at Chundrapoor. Latterly, Her Majesty's ancient, loyal, and faithful petitioners, in the year 1857, in consequence of the disastrous calamities that occurred in Bengal, which were so grievous to the State, made a representation to Colonel Byng, then commanding the regiment, and of our own free will and accord volunteered for general service in Hindostan, to defeat the rebels and suppress the mutiny. Colonel Byng was pleased to forward the representation to his Excellency the Commander-in-chief, Lieutenant-General Sir Patrick Grant, K.C.B., who was graciously pleased to accept of our services, and congratulated and praised the regiment. The same week we received orders to march immediately. At this period the 6th Regiment Light Cavalry was stationed at Jaulnah, in the Deccan. In the month of September, in the monsoon, Her Majesty's loyal and faithful petitioners (leaving their wives and children behind them), with great difficulty swam their horses across the river Wurdah, and with great rapidity reached Nagpore; and, by forced marches from thence to Jubbulpore, they were, on the 14th of the month of November of the same year, engaged with the Bengal rebels The different engagements in which we were, the names of the chief rebels against whom we were engaged, together with the names of the officers who commanded Her Majesty's loyal and faithful subjects, who endured such hardships and privations, are fully detailed in the accompanying memoranda, which we trust your Majesty will graciously condescend to read. His Excellency Lord Clyde, Commander-in-chief in India, having himself witnessed the harassing duties we underwent, and the numerous fights in which we were engaged, both when employed with his own personal column, and with various other columns, in various districts, made honourable mention and praises of us; and Colonel Byng, then commanding the regiment, got the title of C B. In your gracious Majesty's proclamation, dated 1858, it is written that.—'From this date, every person, of whatever race, now in the service of the Honourable East India Company, who has been engaged in supporting the welfare and prosperity of the British power, has now become the servant of Her Majesty Queen of Great Britain.' Her Majesty's petitioners perfectly relied that, by the grace of God and your Majesty's august blessing, we were transferred as the servants of your Majesty, and placing entire confidence in this we did good service, and made the long march back to Bangalore, a distance of 2518 miles On our arrival, Major-General the Honourable A A. Spenser, C B, commanding the Mysore division, inspected us on parade, and in consequence of our having returned from such a distance, was most highly pleased with us, and praised us for our soldier like appearance, alacrity, and steadiness Having made this long march, after being absent so long on foreign service, and having placed entire confidence in the promises that were made to us, that our past loyal and faithful services would be recognised, we trusted that as our forefathers had been honoured so in like manner would we and our offspring. But now suddenly, by the order of your Majesty's Home Government, our regiment has been disbanded, and we have become perplexed and distracted. Moreover, many of our friends and brothers have been discharged, and have thus been separated from us. May it please your Majesty therefore to hear our prayer. It has become the source of great grief to us to have our hopes thus suddenly and entirely cut off, inasmuch as we are the sons of Sepoys who have had for generations, according to the custom of this country, no other way of living save that of being soldiers, and who, in this capacity, have so faithfully served the State for so many generations Up till this time, we confidently believed that we in this regiment, and our offspring in future, would be treated in the same manner as our forefathers had been, while we faithfully continued to obey whatever orders we might receive, and serve wherever we might be required to go. Since Mussulman kings have reigned in Hindostan, our race has always been faithfully employed as cavalry soldiers in their service; and for the last century, since the British rule has existed, we have in the same capacity sacrificed our lives in defence of our flag. We have no native country or home of our own; for the English camp has for generations been our birthplace, our only residence, and our home. We are a race born faithfully to serve with our lives, and devote them for our sovereigns, but in consequence of the regiment's being disbanded, our hopes are suddenly cut off Consequently we are in a state of perplexity and dismay. Moreover, from many causes, and from having made many long and arduous marches, we have become much reduced in circumstances and without pecuniary resources, so much so that we hardly dare venture to relate the same. If it may please your Most Gracious Majesty to confer one favour on your ancient servants (namely, to re-embody our loyal and faithful regiment),[1] your Majesty's humble petitioners will be able to pass their days in ease and happiness, and will for ever, while we continue to live, offer daily prayers for your Majesty's long life and prosperity."

(Signed) By the whole of the native commissioned, non-commissioned, rank and file, and also, at their own request, by all the farriers and trumpeters of the 6th Regiment Madras Light Cavalry.

This petition needs no comment It says all that can be said to show our exact position with the natives of India And I trust that Britain shall candidly and honestly take a review of past policy in India, and ask herself if a policy which may have been justifiable immediately after the suppression of the mutiny, be a

[1] These important words within parentheses were omitted by an oversight when the petition was transmitted to the Commander-in-chief, but are recorded by their request in my official correspondence, in explanation of the "favour" which constituted the prayer of their petition

wise and good policy to be continued in India so as to guarantee future peace and safety.

But to show that any course of policy is wrong is one thing, and a comparatively easy thing. I shall therefore most humbly suggest what course should now be adopted, instead of that which I would like to be superseded And I do take upon myself to make suggestions of this nature, because I know that I would not be faithful either to my country or to India were I not to lay my convictions before the world, and within the reach of the Indian Council It is not only that I have fears as to what may happen any day *in* India, but I have equal fears as to what may happen *to* India.

In my conviction, it would now be well for both Britain and India that Her Majesty the Queen of Britain should afresh make a proclamation that India was made part of England, in order that Englishmen might be enabled to establish peace and equity in India as they exist in England, and that every human being in India therefore was free in the choice of his religion and every matter that regards conscience or matters of mere opinion. This would be as necessary as a matter of form, as that some outward symbol of good faith is current among ourselves in almost all our more important transactions

Then, if natives were made sensible by the Government that it was our wish and determination to do unto them as we would that they should do unto us, they would willingly pay to keep up a government and army so strong as to defy opposition or invasion.

Then, as regards the military department, it would be well to have a thoroughly-equipped and highly-disciplined European and native army entirely under the Commander-in-chief, kept in as few great military stations as possible, and ever ready for any emergency,—that is, for active service in India or in any other part of the world And it should be distinctly known by *every man* in this great army what the regulations of the service make him entitled to receive from the Government while on march, or in cantonments, or in any possible position. Moreover, besides knowing his dues when alive, every man should know clearly what claim his heirs may have on the Government after his death, on account of his service. All the irritations which have been mistakenly called or treated as mutinies in the ever-loyal-at-heart Madras army, with one or two exceptions, have arisen simply from truly trifling pecuniary misunderstandings. The exceptional cases arose from disregarding caste prejudices, such as commencing the march of the 8th Light Cavalry on the very morning of the *Kootbah*, the great annual feast of the Sepoys.

Secondly, It would be well to have a cheap army of irregulars, similar in all respects to that of Mysore, and their head as absolutely under the Governor of

Madras, as I, at the head of the Mysore troops, was under the Commissioner of Mysore. The long-forgotten petition of the 6th Madras Light Cavalry affords a marvellously happy pretext for re-embodying as Sillahdars the four disbanded regiments of Madras cavalry. And as nothing is so prized by any man as his own life, I would willingly stake mine in proof of my conviction of their loyalty. Were I in my old age honoured with the duty of raising four regiments of Queen's Sillahdar horse out of the four regiments of Madras cavalry disbanded so many years ago, I should consider myself more fortunate than had I in 1857 marched with my 2000 Sillahdars and prevented the rising at Sagur.[1] This would *now* be a stroke of policy that would tend to establish good faith between Britain and India, respect for the Government in India, and love for our Queen.[2] It would obliterate all memory of the past, and bury in oblivion those feelings that were engendered by the disbanding of these faithful regiments. For many years, indeed ever since the death of Sir Thomas Munro, the Madras has been a despised army; but no troops exist with a more glorious prestige than the true Madras Maho-

[1] That the rising of Sagur would never have taken place, had I marched with my Sillahdars, is the opinion of one who, in all India, was the most competent to judge, and in whose judgment all who know him, I am certain, would be satisfied.

[2] And never could there be a fitter time than the present, which would be a recognition of the sympathy expressed by India for the recovery of the son and heir of our beloved Queen.

metan *Sowar*. His tale, simply told, is that their Arab chieftain was one of the first Mahometan conquerors of India. He brought them first to Delhi, next to Bejapoor, then to Arcot, where he became Nabob of the Carnatic. He and the English were at war with Hyder Ally of Mysore, when they were transferred to serve under English officers So from time immemorial they are an unconquered race of Arabs.

It was this policy of disbanding, after the suppression of the mutiny, the very men who saved India, inasmuch as they did not join the insurgents, and fought bravely to put them down, that has placed Britain and India on feelings of mutual distrust, which, for the good of both countries, I would like to be annihilated, and see mutual confidence restored. That this was the feeling in India on the subject, the petition alone can abundantly testify, and that this is the feeling in India still, no man who thoroughly knows India, or has the good of both countries at heart, can, with a clear conscience, deny.

As in all matters in which injustice is, or is supposed to be, practised, the feeling against the disbanding of these regiments was not confined to the disbanded alone, but was alike shared by Brahmin and Mahometan throughout the country. Taking all circumstances of their case into consideration, it requires no arguments to prove that this sympathy was general, if not universal.

But were these regiments to be re-embodied, as I have suggested, it is not only that a renewal of perfect confidence in the Government of Britain would be restored, but such a policy would serve to gratify the Brahmins, who above all men love peace and security, and who looked on the Sepoys as their natural protectors even under the Government of Britain, as was really the case And let it not be said that the pleasing of the Brahmins is a matter of no moment to Britain, while the Brahmin is possessed of almost matchless intelligence, ingenuity, and craft to mould and wield the wills of the Sepoys either for good or for evil, who are more accustomed to action than thought The one race is subtle, cunning, scheming; the other brave, hardy, and constant; and thus the one race has almost unlimited control over the other. The two races are as head and hand to each other.

It is almost painful to rehearse that I have heard oftener than once, "Let India go, Britain would be better without India." Thanks, however, to the united wisdom and intelligence that really controls so large a section of the human race, such an opinion is far from being theirs. It requires no gift of prophecy to see that India, instead of decreasing in importance to Britain, is daily becoming more important to Britain in the eyes of all classes of men. The history of India under British domination hitherto, is that of a vast field for political, military, and mercantile enterprise; but still there is room for greater conquests by the Christian, the philanthropist, and the philosopher. In a word, India *now* is interesting to all these classes of men.

It is not with less pain that I have heard it said that European force alone can keep India safe, and true to Britain. Indeed, British force has done and can do a great deal, but pure physical force never did nor can keep India in subjection for a day, and far less can it keep India true to Britain in the event of an invasion by any foreign country. But British moral force, tempered with Christian charity, can make India safe and true to Britain for ever. No wise man could ever dream of establishing truth and fidelity by force. And it is on this account that I do humbly recommend the adoption of all those amicable measures of policy that will eventually establish truth and fidelity, and the extermination of everything that has the very appearance of force or mistrust between Britain and India.

Indeed, British force, its pure physical force, is necessary for the preservation of India to Indians themselves. And the natives of India know and thankfully acknowledge this, and they cannot be too often reminded how it was British force that saved them and protected them from the worst of all enemies —internal discord. Before the establishment of British power in India there was nothing but feud, bloodshed, surprise, rapine, and every form of anarchy and insecurity, arising from contention between a variety of usurpers and chiefs of the country. It required the strong hand of Britain to put down and keep in subjection these adventurous tyrants and exterminators of everything that bore the character of human or divine. And the day that India forgets her obligations to Britain on this score, she may learn, when too late, the value of the truly humanizing influence, amid much seemingly discordant elements, of British sovereignty and government in India.

But notwithstanding these blessings of peace and security which the native of India has enjoyed under the sceptre of Britain, I would insist on that wisdom and moderation of rule in every way possible, that the native would be compelled to feel a force superior to any outward force, as emanating from, and resident in, the British character. This force of character in peace is just as characteristic of the Briton as his force of character in war, and the only difference is, that in his own bluntness he is unconscious of its value, or even that he himself is the possessor of it. And if *he* is justly applauded and rewarded who restores and establishes peace by the strong hand of necessity, through the shedding of blood, how much more deserving of commendation and reward is he who preserves peace unbroken with a power stronger than the sword, and does not necessitate the spilling of blood? May this be the continual aim of every true Briton; and hereby prove to all men that his character is consistent with his religion, whose first announcement was to introduce "peace on earth and good-will towards men."

SINCE the printing of the above, a remarkable and unexpected confirmation of the views embodied in it has been received in an official Minute of the present Commander-in-Chief in India, Lord Napier of Magdala, dated 14th November 1870.

Perhaps there is no greater living authority on the subject, and I therefore make no apology for reproducing it His words are these —

"In looking," says his Lordship, "to our general position in India, I cannot find ground for believing that we may neglect any means of maintaining our supremacy, or disarm, without risk, in a fancied security It appears to me that we never had less hold on the affections of the people than at present I do not at all attribute this to the income-tax, of which we should have heard very little if Europeans had been exempt The cause is, I believe, much deeper The class of European officials who made India their home, and identified themselves with the people, is represented by a very few such men as Colonel Ramsay, of Kemaon. The remembrance of the benefits which we conferred on the people of the parts of India which we relieved from oppression and misrule has passed away with the people of those days; the present generation only consider their present restraints and the obligations imposed on them, and the more educated and ambitious look for a larger share of places of influence and emoluments than they now possess The Mahometan movement, though the scope of its objects and intentions has not been fully brought to light, shows a much wider extent and combination than we have hitherto appreciated.

"In spite," he adds, "of the vigilance of our Custom-house officers, we may be sure that a considerable influx of superior weapons finds its way into the country, and that in any future strife the soldiers of native States will be found to have shared in the general improvements of the implements of warfare, and should the misfortüne of disturbance arise we shall still require the support of a preponderance of artillery to compensate for deficiency of numbers compared to the vast populations and the extent of country which we have to control, and the widespread and various interests we have to protect If an external enemy should appear on our frontier, there will not be wanting many within our own territories ready to seek advantage from a change, or to avenge some long-cherished grievance or animosity"

Lord Napier has done great service to the British Government in his having thus timely and without reserve given, in his opinion, a true statement of our position in India; and the Indian Council have acted with admirable good policy in laying his Minute before the public, whatever minor politicians may think to the contrary. To be forewarned is to be forearmed; and besides, the making public of any secret movements has a tendency to render them abortive. It is a poor policy that has to skulk in the dark. It will be a poor day for Britain when she must have recourse to any policy but candour and the most open publicity. Such has been her policy even in her mistakes, and this, perhaps above all things, is her chief characteristic among the nations of the earth. Let us not therefore shrink from our duty because a few politicians may be too faint-hearted to look it in the face. A gentleman of wide and grasping intellect (Professor Seeley of Cambridge), in his late lecture on the "British Empire," in the Philosophical Institution, Edinburgh, is reported to have thus expressed himself:—

"He described Britain as a conquering nation, and spoke in illustration of her great Indian and Colonial empires He referred to the immense questions which the government of these empires involved—questions the importance of which the present ignorant state of public opinion could not grasp Inability or unwillingness to face the difficulties surrounding our colonial empire was fast drifting us into separation —a catastrophe which was in every way to be deprecated. For England to lose her cosmopolitan character would be a great retrogression, and to prevent this every one could contribute something All of them should leave off the disagreeable practice of referring perpetually to the cost of the colonies, and respond more to their loyalty, for if the British Empire should be disrupted, every cold sneer now at the interested loyalty of our colonies would be a deadly blow aimed at the future welfare of our country and mankind."

The following startling assertions which have appeared in the public prints should not be overlooked without serious consideration. They are not the thoughts of a solitary individual. I am almost convinced that there are thousands in Britain to-day who hold that they have a prophetic significance.

"ENGLAND AND RUSSIA.

"The *Morning Advertiser* notes that 'step by step Russia is marching towards her long-coveted goal. The neutralization of the Black Sea is set aside, the Crimea is to be fortified all round, the military power of the Czar in Central Asia is being consolidated for that purpose The fact of our being without allies is so new and strange to us, that the country has not yet realized its significance In the Crimean War the interests of France were identical with our own, and we had her for an ally against Russia In the last 'great war' we had all Europe for our allies against Bonaparte So in the great wars with Louis XIV we had powerful allies with us, such as the German armies, under one of the ablest generals in modern times—Prince Eugene Our army has always been so small that through the wars which ended in 1815, when our armaments were at their height, our force did not exceed 40,000 men. And now we stand alone against Russia, whose armies for attacking Turkey and India exceed a million of men'"—*Courant, April* 1*st*, 1872

II.

ORIGIN AND STATE OF THE INDIAN ARMY.

I SHALL now introduce a short account of the origin and state of the armies of the three Presidencies, and, as an eminent writer says, this account "is not a specious theory, but an accumulation of facts, which we require to guide our judgment through the difficult, and, we may say, the awful task of governing the vast dominions which we have acquired in the East, and none are more important than those which throw light upon the character of that army, by whose valour and attachment the great conquest has been principally achieved, and without whose continued fidelity it cannot be preserved."

I quote this admirable account from the pages of the *Quarterly Review* of 1817, and Sir Mark Cubbon, in giving it to me to read, many years ago, stated that the eminent reviewer was no less an authority than Sir John Malcolm.

"The decided preference which a great proportion of the inhabitants of India have shown towards the rule of the British Government, originated in several causes, but in none more than an observation of the courage and discipline of its troops, and the comparative superiority both in regard to the justice and permanence of its civil institutions. Nations wearied out with the dissensions and oppressions of barbarous and rival chiefs, found (to use the Oriental phrase) repose under the shadow of its protection, and the great mass of the people have been benefited in their condition by the extension of its power—but their princes have almost all fallen The territories of the monarchs who opposed, and who supported this government, have shared the same fate—all have been absorbed in one vortex;—the only difference has been, that the one has perished by a sudden and violent death, while the dissolution of the other has been comparatively easy and gradual. It is difficult to repress those feelings which the past view of this picture is calculated to excite; one of the most natural and legitimate sentiments of the human mind leads it to regard that power which has been long established in ancient and noble families with respect, if not veneration. It is the great link of order in every society, particularly in those where the rule is simple and despotic. We are compelled by the impulse of this feeling to regard every species of usurpation with disgust, but above all, that of strangers, who appear to the general observer to have subdued the natives of one of the finest portions of the earth, with no view but the sordid and inglorious one of rendering their land a source of profit, or at least using that power which its possession gave them, to protect a profitable commerce. British India cannot be considered as a colony. Its rank is that of a dependent empire,—and though the chain of connexion by which it is preserved in subjection may want some of those links which have ever been deemed essential to the maintenance of power, there are in its constitution advantages of no ordinary magnitude. One of the most striking is, that it contains fewer of those elements, which produce acts of violence and injustice, than any other State in the universe. Its governors are mere ministers, who are controlled by their superiors in England, and checked (if they attempt any unwise or illegal exercise of their authority) by their colleagues in power in India.

"The character of the government they serve, and of that they preside over, precludes those ebullitions of personal ambition which have so often hastened the downfall of other kingdoms; and we believe that the benefit derived from that calmness and exclusive attention to the public interest, with which their peculiar condition enables them to exercise their sovereign functions, is the chief ground upon which we can build any expectation of the duration of the empire we have established. This empire has probably not yet reached its zenith—we are aware of all the dangers of its increase. Like the circle in the water, the very trace of our power will, in all probability be lost in expansion; but we are among those who doubt the possibility of fixing the limits of our career. Every effort, however, should be made to retard it. As European politicians we may be allowed to express our fear, that the local government of India, throughout all its branches, is impelled, by its very nature, to promote change and the aggrandizement of the State Public officers, from the Governor-General to the lowest of those who hold stations of any consequence, must, from the ephemeral character of their power, have an anxiety to recommend themselves, during the short hour of their authority, to their superiors, and men of the most distinguished virtue and talent often desire action with an ardour that makes them more ready to combat than to attend to the cold dictates of moderation and prudence. To the Indian government in England, which is, on the other hand, perhaps too free from the influence of similar motives, belongs the task of repressing and keeping within due limits that natural spirit of ambition, which the minds of those imbibe whose attention for any period is exclusively fixed on India. But to render this check efficient, it is necessary that those in whose hands it is placed should act with full knowledge, and with the most enlarged views; otherwise the end will be defeated. If orders grounded on imperfect knowledge, narrow views, and general maxims of rule, which are, perhaps, inapplicable to the actual condition of the empire, and to passing events, are sent to India, they will, they must be, evaded or neglected. The safety of the State requires that they should—and after all, though we may, and ought, to use every endeavour to retard, if we cannot arrest, the growth of our Eastern possessions, still events will occur to mock every attempt to reduce our conduct in the pursuit of this policy to any exact laws. For let us suppose for a moment, that those employed to govern abroad were subdued into the most passive and unimpassioned instruments that the lovers of implicit obedience could desire, can we make the plunderer renounce his love of plunder—the vanquished forgive his conqueror—or the faithless maintain his engagements? To us the progress of our power in India appears, in a great degree, to be the triumph of civilisation and knowledge, over rudeness and ignorance. States whose territories adjoin, whose subjects are the same in language and manners, and who are governed on such opposite principles, cannot avoid collision; and the English have always been in a situation in India that forbade any compromise of a power, the peculiar character of which has required a constant accession to that impression of superiority upon which its existence depends. This principle, or rather necessity of action, for such it would appear, has propelled us forward, till our empire has attained its present magnitude, and we contemplate, with equal astonishment and awe, the political phenomenon of a few strangers, whose ships have conveyed them from a distant island in Europe, exercising sovereign sway over 400,000 square miles of the finest part of the continent of Asia, and claiming as their indefeasible right the allegiance of fifty millions of the inhabitants of that quarter of the globe.

"One of the principal means by which this extensive conquest has been made, and the one to which we must chiefly trust for its defence, is the Native army of the East India Company, which at present exceeds 150,000 effective men The work before us[1] gives the best account we have met with of the origin and formation of that part of this great army, which more particularly belongs to Bengal; but we have made it our duty to seek other sources of information, that we may be able to take the most comprehensive view of a subject so vital to our Eastern empire we shall endeavour to trace the progress of the native troops at Madras and Bombay, before we examine the facts brought before us by Captain Williams. A combined view of the whole may suggest some reflections on the means which appear best calculated to maintain the efficiency, and preserve the attachment of the Indian army

[1] Captain Williams's *Historical Account of the Rise and Progress of the Bengal Native Infantry* London, 1817.

"Though Bombay was the first possession which the English obtained in the East, the establishment on that island was for a very long period on too limited a scale to maintain more than its European garrison, and a few companies of disciplined Sepoys. On the coast of Coromandel, which became towards the middle of the last century a scene of warfare between the English and French, who mutually aided and received support from the princes of that quarter, the natives of India were first instructed in European discipline During the siege of Madras, which took place in A D. 1746, a number of peons, a species of irregular infantry armed with swords and spears, or matchlocks, were enlisted for the occasion. To those some English officers were attached, among whom a young gentleman of the civil service, of the name of Haliburton, was the most distinguished. This gentleman, who had been rewarded with the commission of a lieutenant, was employed in the ensuing year in training a small corps of natives in the European manner. He did not, however, live to perfect that system which he appears to have first introduced into the Madras service

"'It was by one of our own Sepoys,' the Council of Fort St David observe, in a despatch dated the 2d September 1748, in which they pass an eulogium on the character of Mr Haliburton, 'that he had the misfortune to be killed, who shot him upon his reprimanding him for some offence The poor gentleman,' they add, 'died next day, and the villain did not live so long, for his comrades that stood by cut him to pieces immediately.'

"It appears from other authorities, that the first Sepoys who were raised by the English, were either Mahomedans, or Hindoos of very high caste, being chiefly rajpoots; and the event we have related marked the two strongest feelings of the minds of these classes,—resentment for real or supposed injury, and attachment to their leader. The name of Mr. Haliburton was long cherished by the Madras native troops, and about twenty years ago, on an examination of old grants, some veterans, wearing medals, appeared as claimants who called themselves Saheb Ra Sepoy, or Haliburton's soldiers. One of the first services on which the regular Sepoys of Madras were employed, was the defence of Arcot, A.D. 1751. The particulars of that siege, which forms a remarkable feature in the life of the celebrated Clive, have been given by an eloquent and faithful historian;[1] but he has not informed us of one occurrence that took place, and which, as it illustrates the character of the Indian soldiers, well merited to be preserved. When provisions were very low, the Hindoo Sepoys entreated their commander to allow them to boil the rice (the only food left) for the whole garrison. 'Your English soldiers,' they said, 'can eat from our hands, though we cannot from theirs; we will allot as their share

[1] "Orme.

every grain of the rice, and subsist ourselves by drinking the water in which it has been boiled.' We have received this remarkable anecdote from an authority we cannot doubt, as it refers to the most unexceptionable contemporary witnesses

"During all the wars of Clive, of Lawrence, of Smith, and of Coote, the Sepoys of Madras continued to display the same valour and attachment. In the years 1780, 81, and 82, they suffered hardships of a nature almost unparalleled. There was hardly a corps that was not twenty months in arrears They were supported, it is true, by a daily allowance of rice, but this was not enough to save many of their families from being the victims of that dreadful famine which during these years wasted the Company's dominions in India. Their fidelity never gave way in this hour of extreme trial, and they repaid with gratitude and attachment the kindness and the consideration with which they were treated by their European officers, who, being few in number, but, generally speaking, very efficient, tried every means that could conciliate the regard, excite the pride, or stimulate the valour of those they commanded.

"In the campaigns of 1790 and 91, against Tippoo Sultaun, the Sepoys of this establishment showed their usual zeal and courage, but the number of European troops which were now intermixed with them lessened their opportunities of distinguishing themselves, and though improved in discipline, they perhaps fell in their own estimation. The native army, in some degree, became a secondary one, and the pride of those of whom it was composed was lowered We are neither questioning the necessity of the increased number of His Majesty's troops, which were employed in India at this period, or the propriety of allotting to their superior strength and active courage services of the greatest danger, and consequently of pre-eminent honour we only speak to the effect which the change made in the minds of the native army. The campaigns of Lord Cornwallis and General Meadows were certainly not inferior, either in their operations or results, to those of Sir Eyre Coote, and every officer can tell how differently they are regarded by the Sepoys, who served in both, the latter may bring to their memory the distresses and hardships which they suffered, and perhaps the recollection of children who perished from famine; but it is associated with a sense of their own importance, at that period, to the government they served, with the pride of fidelity and patient valour. The pictures of these three distinguished leaders are in the great room of the Exchange at Madras To that (we speak of ten years ago, 1807), when a battalion comes into garrison, the old Sepoys lead their families. *Wallis* and *Meadows* (these are the names by which the two first commanders are known to them) are pointed out as great and brave chiefs;

but it is to the image of their favourite, Coote, the pilgrimage is made, and the youngest of their children are taught to pay a respect bordering on devotion to this revered leader.

"In the year 1796 new regulations were introduced into the Indian army, the whole form of which was in fact changed. Instead of single battalions of a thousand men, commanded by a captain who was selected from the European corps in the Hon Company's service, and a subaltern to each company, they were formed into regiments of two battalions, to which officers were appointed of the same rank and nearly of the same number as to a battalion in the service of His Majesty The good effects of this change, as far as related to the temper and attachment of the native army of Fort St. George, have been questioned by an officer of that establishment, who was from local experience well qualified to judge[1] That the appearance and discipline of these troops have been improved, there is no doubt, and they have, in the campaign against Seringapatam, in 1799, and in the recent war with the Mahrattas, shown their usual patience and courage; but events have occurred to prove that their affections were not only capable of being alienated from their European officers, but that they could become their murderers. It is not here meant to enter into the particulars of the mutiny at

[1] " *Vide* Malcolm's *Political History of India*, p 495.

Vellore, which came like a shock to dispel the charm of half a century, and to show by what a tenure our empire is held, but we are certainly disposed to think, with the officer to whom we have alluded, that this event could not have taken place had the ties which formerly existed in the native army not been much weakened, if not entirely broken. Of what has since occurred, we forbear to speak, but we are assured that time, and the efforts of great wisdom, can alone afford a hope of a radical cure to the deep wounds that have been inflicted.

"The general history of the native army of Fort St. George is short. Sepoys were first disciplined, as has been stated, on that establishment, in 1748, they were at that period, and for some time afterwards, in independent companies, under subadars or native captains. Mahomed Esof, one of the most distinguished of those officers, rose by his talents and courage to the general command of the whole, and the name of this hero, for such he was, occurs almost as often in the page of the English historian[1] of India as that of Lawrence and Clive. As the numbers of the native army increased, the form changed. In A.D. 1766, we find ten battalions of 1000 men each, and three European officers to each corps. In 1770, there were eighteen battalions of similar strength; and in 1784 the number of this army had increased to 2000 native cavalry and

[1] "Orme

28,000 infantry. A considerable reduction was made at this period; but subsequent wars and conquests have caused a great increase, and the present effective strength of the native army of Fort St George consists of eight regiments of cavalry, and twenty-four regiments or forty-eight battalions of native infantry There are, besides, several troops of horse artillery, some battalions of gun lascars, and a very large invalid establishment

"A few remarks on the appearance and conduct of this army, with some anecdotes of remarkable individuals, will fully illustrate its character, and convey to the uninformed reader a just idea of the elements of which it is composed

"The native cavalry of Fort St. George was originally raised by the Nabob of the Carnatic.[1] The first corps embodied into a regiment under the command of European officers, on the suggestion of General Joseph Smith, served in the campaign of 1768, in the Mysore. From 1771 to 1776, the cavalry force was greatly augmented, but then again declined both in numbers and efficiency. The proportion that was retained, nominally in the service of the Nabob, but actually in that of the Company, served in the campaigns of 1780, 81, 82, and 83, and was formally

[1] This appears to be a mistake Native officers and cavalry Sepoys assured me often that they were as of pure Arab descent as the Nabob of the Carnatic Their ancestors followed his ancestor, their chief, from Arabia to Delhi, thence to Beejapore, and from that to Arcot, when he became Nabob of the Carnatic, etc. etc —A. MACLEOD

transferred, with the European officers attached to it, to the Company's service in 1784. The prospect of fortune, which the liberality of an Indian prince offered, attracted to this corps many active and enterprising European officers, and the favour which a native court extended to its choicest troops, filled the ranks of its regiments of regular cavalry with the prime of the Mahomedan youth[1] of the Carnatic. When this corps was in the service of the Nabob of the Carnatic, though it was often very highly distinguished, the intrigues of a venal court, and irregular payments, caused frequent mutinies. Since it has been transferred to the Company's establishment, a period of more than thirty years, its career has been one of faithful service, and of brilliant achievement, unstained by any example that we can recollect of disaffection or of defeat. The two severest trials of the courage and discipline of this corps were at Assaye and Vellore, in both these services they were associated with the 19th dragoons.

"The distinguished commander[2] of that gallant regiment had, from the day of its arrival in India, laboured to establish the ties of mutual and cordial regard between the European and native soldiers.

1 "There cannot be men more suited, from their frame and disposition, for the duty of light cavalry, than those of which this corps is composed. They are, generally speaking, from five feet five to five feet ten inches in height, of light but active make Their strength is preserved and improved by moderation in their diet, and by exercises common to the military tribe, and which are calculated to increase the muscular force

2 "The present General Sir John Floyd, Bart

His success was complete—his own fame, while he remained in India, was promoted by their combined efforts—and the friendship which he established and which had continued for many years, was, after his departure, consummated upon the plains of Assaye At the most critical moment of a battle which ranks amongst the hardest fought of those that have been gained by the illustrious Wellington, the British dragoons, when making their extremest efforts, saw their Asiatic fellow-soldiers 'keep pace for pace, and blow for every blow.' A more arduous task awaited the latter, when the battalions of native infantry which formed the garrison of Vellore were led by the infatuation of the moment to rise upon and murder the Europeans of that garrison. The fidelity of the native cavalry did not shrink from this severe trial, and after the gates of the fortress were blown open, their sabres were as deeply[1] stained as those of the English dragoons with the blood of their misguided and guilty countrymen.

"But a few authentic anecdotes of some of the most distinguished individuals of the native cavalry of Madras will show better than volumes the high spirit which pervades that corps.

"In the campaign of 1791, when Secunder Beg, one of the oldest subadars of the native cavalry, was riding at a little distance in the flank of his troop,

[1] "We state this fact upon the high authority of a respectable officer, who belonged to the 19th dragoons, and was with them on this memorable occasion

two or three horsemen of Tippoo's army, favoured by some brushwood, came suddenly upon him; the combat had hardly commenced, when the son of the subadar, who was a havildar or serjeant in the same regiment, flew to his father's aid, and slew the foremost of his opponents; the others fled, but nothing could exceed the rage of the old man at his son's conduct; he put him instantly under a guard, and insisted upon his being brought to condign punishment for quitting his ranks without leave. It was with the greatest difficulty that Colonel Floyd, who commanded the force, could reconcile him to the disgrace he conceived he had suffered (to use his own expression) 'from his enemy being taken from him by a presumptuous boy in front of his regiment.'

"Cawder Beg, late subadar of the Fourth Regiment, may be deemed throughout his life as one of the most distinguished officers of the native cavalry of Madras. In 1790, he was attached to Colonel Floyd as an orderly subadar, when that officer, who had been reconnoitring with a small detachment, was attacked by a considerable body of the enemy's horse Nothing but the greatest exertions of every individual could have saved the party from being cut off. Those of Cawder Beg were the most conspicuous, and they received a reward of which he was proud to the last hour of his life; an English sabre was sent to him, with the name of Colonel Floyd upon it, and an inscription stating that it was the reward of valour.

But personal courage was the least quality of Cawder Beg; his talents eminently fitted him for the exercise of military command. During the campaign of 1799, it was essential to prevent the enemy's looties, a species of Cossack horse, from penetrating between the columns and the rear-guard, and plundering any part of that immense train of provisions and luggage which it was necessary to carry to Seringapatam. Cawder Beg, with two or three of his relations from the native cavalry, and a select body of infantry, were placed under the orders of Captain Malcolm,[1] who was then political representative with the army of the subah of the Deckan, and commanded a considerable body of the troops of that prince. Captain Malcolm, who had applied for Cawder Beg on account of his reputation, prevailed upon Meer Allum, the leader of the subah's forces, to place a corps of 2000 of his best regular horse under the subadar's orders. Two days after the corps was formed, an orderly trooper came up to Captain Malcolm, and told him that Cawder Beg was engaged with some of the enemy's horsemen. Captain Malcolm hastened to the spot, with some alarm for the result, and determined, if Cawder Beg was victor, to reprove him most severely for a conduct so unsuited to the station in which he had been placed. The fears he entertained for his safety were soon dispelled, as he saw him advancing on foot with two swords in his hand, which

[1] "Now Sir John Malcolm

he hastened to present to Captain Malcolm, begging at the same time he would restrain his indignation at his apparent rashness, till he heard his reasons; then, speaking to him aside, he said—

"'Though the general of the Nizam's army was convinced by your statement of my competence to the command you have intrusted me with, I observed that the high-born and high-titled leaders of the horse he placed under my orders looked at my close jacket,[1] straight pantaloons, and European boots, with contempt, and thought themselves disgraced by being told to obey me, I was therefore tempted, on seeing a well-mounted horseman of Tippoo's challenge their whole line, to accept a combat, which they declined I promised not to use fire-arms, and succeeded in cutting him down; a relation came to avenge his death, I wounded him, and have brought him prisoner You will (he added, smiling) hear a good report of me at the durbar (court) of Meer Allum this evening—and the service will go on better for what has passed,—and I promise most sacredly to fight no more single combats'

"When Captain Malcolm went in the evening to visit the Nizam's gurwal, he found at his tent a number of the principal chiefs, and among others, those that had been with Cawder Beg; with whose praises he was assailed from every quarter. 'He was,' they said, 'a perfect hero, a Rustum,[2] it was an honour to be commanded by so great a leader' The consequence was, as the subadar had anticipated—that the different chiefs who were placed under him vied in respect

[1] "The native troops in the English service wear a uniform very like that of Europeans.

[2] The Persian Hercules

and obedience; and so well were the incessant efforts of this body directed, that scarcely a load of grain was lost, hardly a day passed that the activity and stratagem of Cawder Beg did not delude some of the enemy's plunderers to their destruction

"It would fill a volume to give a minute account of the actions of this gallant officer; he was the native aid-de-camp of General Dugald Campbell, when that officer reduced the ceded districts;[1] he attended Sir Arthur Wellesley (the present Duke of Wellington) in the campaign of 1803, and was employed by that officer in the most confidential manner. At the end of this campaign, during which he had several opportunities of distinguishing himself, Cawder Beg, who had received a pension from the English Government, and whose pride was flattered by being created an omrah[2] of the Deckan by the Nizam, retired, but he did not long enjoy the distinction he had obtained,—he died in 1806, worn out with the excessive fatigue to which he had for many years exposed himself.

"The body-guard of the governor of Madras, which consists of about one hundred men, has always been a very select corps, and the notice and attention with which both the native officers and men of the corps

[1] "These districts, which were ceded to the English Government by the treaty of Seringapatam, in 1799, lie between Mysore proper, and the territories of the Subah of the Deckan

[2] "He received the title of Cawder Nuaz Khan, or Cawder the favourite lord

have invariably been treated, may be adduced as one of the causes which have led to its obtaining distinction in every service on which it has been employed.

"On the 13th of May 1791, Lord Cornwallis returned his thanks in the warmest terms to this small corps and its gallant commanding officer, Captain Alexander Grant, for a charge made upon the enemy. It obtained still further distinction under Captain James Grant, the brother of its former commander, when employed in the year 1801 against the Poligars, a race of warlike men who inhabit the southern part of the Madras territory. There are, indeed, few examples of a more desperate and successful charge than was made during that service by this small corps, upon a phalanx of resolute pikemen, more than double its own numbers, and the behaviour of Shaikh Ibrahim, the senior subadar (a native captain), on that occasion, merits to be commemorated.

"This officer, who was alike remarkable for his gallantry and unrivalled skill as a horseman, anticipated, from his experience of the enemy, all that would happen. He told Captain Grant what he thought would be the fate of those who led the charge, at the same moment that he urged it, and heard with animated delight the resolution of his commander to attempt an exploit which was to reflect such glory on the corps. The leaders of the body-guard, and almost one-third of its number, fell, as was expected; but the shock broke the order of their opponents, and they obtained a complete victory. Shaikh Ibrahim was pierced with several pikes; one was in the throat; he held his hand to this, as if eager to keep life till he asked the fate of Captain Grant. The man of whom he inquired pointed to that officer, who was lying on the ground, and apparently dead, with a pike through his lungs, the subadar, with an expression of regret that he had disdained to show for his own fate, pulled the pike from the wound, and instantly expired. His character and his behaviour in the last moment of his existence are fully described in the following General Order, which was issued on this occasion by the government of Fort St George:—

"'A rare combination of talents has rendered the character of Shaikh Ibrahim familiar to the officers of the army to cool decision and daring valour, he added that sober judgment and those honourable sentiments, that raised him far above the level of his rank in life An exploit of uncommon energy and personal exertion terminated his career, and the last effort of his voice breathed honour, attachment, and fidelity

"'The Governor in Council, desirous of showing to the army his Lordship's[1] sense of the virtue and attainments which have rendered the death of this native officer a severe loss to the service, has been pleased to confer on his family a pension equal to the pay of a subadar of the body-guard,

[1] "Lord Clive (the present Lord Powis) was at this period Governor of Madras, and it is but justice to that nobleman to state that virtue, talent, or valour, either in European or native, were certain under his administration of attaining distinction and reward.

being 30 pagodas per month, and his Lordship has further directed that a certificate to this effect, translated into Persian and Hindostanee, may be presented to the family, as a record of the gift, and a tribute to the memory of the brave subadar Shaikh Ibrahim.'

"The posthumous praise given to Shaikh Ibrahim appeared to have inspired others with a desire to share his fate, that they might attain his fame. A jemadar of the same corps, some days afterwards, being appointed with a few select men to watch a road, where it was thought the chief whom they were attacking might try to escape with one or two followers, determined when a whole column came out to make an attempt against its leader, and such was the surprise at seeing five or six horsemen ride into a body of between two or three hundred men, that he had cut down the chief before they recovered from their astonishment; he succeeded in riding out of the column, but was soon afterwards shot. He had, when he meditated this attack, sent a person to inform Captain J. Grant (who had recovered of his wounds) of his intention 'The captain will discover,' he observed, 'that there are more Shaikh Ibrahims than one in the body-guard. Captain Grant, when the service was over, erected tombs over these gallant officers: a constant lamp is kept at them, which is supported by a trifling monthly donation from every man in the body-guard, and the noble spirit of the corps is perpetuated by the contemplation of these regimental shrines (for such they may be termed) of heroic valour.

"Shaikh Moheedeen, a subadar of the body-guard of Madras, who was one of the first officers appointed to the corps of native horse artillery recently raised on that establishment, accompanied Sir John Malcolm to Persia, and was left with a detachment of his corps under the command of Captain Lindsay, to aid in instructing the Persians in military tactics This small body of men and their gallant European commander were engaged in several campaigns in Georgia, and their conduct has obtained, not only for the subadar, but for all the men of his party, marked honours and reward, both from the Persian government and their own. Their exertions received additional importance from the scene on which they acted, for it is not easy to calculate the future benefits which may result from the display of the superior courage and discipline of the native soldiers of India on the banks of the Araxes

"The native infantry of Madras is generally composed of Mahomedans and Hindoos of good caste: at its first establishment none were enlisted but men of high military tribes. In the progress of time a considerable change took place, and natives of every description were enrolled in the service. Though some corps that were almost entirely formed of the lowest and most despised races of men obtained considerable reputation, it was feared their encouragement might produce disgust, and particularly when they gained, as they frequently did, the rank of officers. Orders were in consequence given to recruit from none but the most respectable classes of society, and many consider the regular and orderly behaviour of these men as one of the benefits which have resulted from this system.

"The infantry Sepoy of Madras is rather a small man, but he is of an active make, and capable of undergoing great fatigue upon a very slender diet. We find no man arrive at greater precision in all his military exercises; his moderation, his sobriety, his patience, give him a steadiness that is almost unknown to Europeans, but though there exists in this body of men a fitness to attain mechanical perfection as soldiers, there are no men whose mind it is of more consequence to study. The most marked general feature of the character of the natives of India is a proneness to obedience, accompanied by a great susceptibility of good or bad usage; and there are few in that country who are more imbued with these feelings than the class of which we are now treating. The Sepoys of Madras, when kindly treated, have invariably shown great attachment[1] to the service; and

[1] "In old corps that have been chiefly recruited within the territories which have been long in the possession of the Company, desertion is of very rare occurrence

"The first battalion of the third native infantry marched in 1803 from

when we know that this class of men can be brought, without harshness or punishment, to the highest discipline, we neither can nor ought to have any toleration for those who pursue a different system; and the Commander-in-chief is unfit for his station who grants his applause to the mere martinet, and forgets, in his intemperate zeal, that no perfection, in appearance and discipline, can make amends for the loss of the temper and attachment of the native soldiers under his command.

"We discover in the pages of Orme many examples of that patient endurance of privations and fatigue, and that steady valour which has since characterized the native infantry of Fort St. George. Their conduct in the war against Hyder Ally in 1766, was such as justly to entitle them to admiration. In the battle of Trinomalee and Molwaggle they displayed all the qualifications of good and steady soldiers, and it was during this war that the fifth battalion of native infantry, commanded by Captain Calvert, distinguished itself by the defence of Ambore, and obtained the honour of bearing a representation of that mountain fortress on one of its standards. To the campaigns of Sir Eyre Coote we have already alluded, and have spoken of the unshaken fidelity which the Sepoys of Madras evinced at that trying juncture; but if a

near Madura, of which district and Trichinopoly a great proportion of its men were natives, to the banks of the Taptee, a distance of above a thousand miles, without one desertion.

moment was to be named when the existence of the British power depended upon its native troops, we should fix upon the battle of Portonovo. Driven to the sea-shore, attacked by an enemy exulting in recent success,[1] confident in his numbers, and strong in the terror of his name; every circumstance combined that could dishearten the small body of men on whom the fate of the war depended not a heart shrunk from the trial. Of the European troops it is of course superfluous to speak; but all the native battalions appear, from every account of the action, to have been entitled to equal praise on this memorable occasion; and it is difficult to say whether they were most distinguished when suffering with a patient courage under a heavy cannonade, when receiving and repulsing the shock of the flower of Hyder's cavalry, or when attacking in their turn the troops of that monarch, who, baffled in all his efforts, retreated from this field of anticipated conquest with the loss of his most celebrated commander, and thousands of his bravest soldiers.

[1] "The defeat of Colonel Baillie's detachment which occurred at the commencement of this war This defeat has been variously attributed to bad arrangements in the general plans of the campaign, to mismanagement on the part of the commanding officer, and to the misconduct of the native troops It is probable all these causes combined to produce this great misfortune, but we must recollect that the native battalions that were chiefly accused of bad behaviour on this occasion were raw levies who had never before seen service, and most of whom had hardly been in the army a sufficient time to be disciplined. The men composing these corps had been hastily raised in the Circars, or northern possessions of Madras, and their conduct created a prejudice (which experience has since proved to be unjust) against recruits from this quarter

"It would exceed our limits to dwell upon the different actions in the war against Tippoo and the Mahrattas, in which the Madras Sepoys signalized themselves; we shall therefore content ourselves with some anecdotes of corps and individuals which appear calculated to give a fair impression of the general character of this class of the defenders of our empire in India.

"The natives of India have, generally speaking, a rooted dislike to the sea, and when we consider the great privations and hardships to which Hindoos of high caste are subject on a long voyage, during which some of them, from prejudices of caste, subsist solely on parched grain, we feel less surprise at the occasional mutinies which have been caused by orders for their embarkation than at the zeal and attachment they have often shown upon such trying occasions.

"A mutiny had occurred in the 9th battalion when ordered to embark for Bombay in 1779 or 1780, which, however, had been quelled by the spirit and decision of its commandant, Captain Kelly. A more serious result had accompanied a similar order for the embarkation of some companies of a corps in the northern Circars, who, when they came to Vizagapatam, the port where they were to take shipping, had risen upon their European officers, and in their violence shot all except one or two who escaped on board the vessel appointed to carry their men.

"These events rendered Government averse to a repetition of experiments which had proved so dangerous; but in the year 1795, when the island of Ceylon and the possessions of the Dutch in the eastern seas were to be reduced, Lord Hobart,[1] who was then governor of Fort St George, made a successful appeal to the zeal and attachment of the native troops, who volunteered in corps for foreign service.

"A still greater call for men was necessary when an army was formed in 1797 for the attack of Manilla, and many of the best battalions in the service showed a forwardness to be employed on this expedition. Among these, one of the most remarkable for its appearance and discipline was a battalion of the Twenty-second Regiment. This fine corps was commanded by Lieutenant-Colonel James Oram,[2] an officer not more distinguished for his personal zeal and gallantry than for a thorough knowledge of the men under his command, whose temper he had completely preserved, at the same time that he had imparted to them the highest perfection in their dress and discipline. When he proposed to his corps on parade to

[1] "Lord Hobart (afterwards Earl of Buckinghamshire) was very successful in inspiring zeal in every branch of the government under his charge, and his attention was peculiarly directed to the conciliation of the natives The local information he acquired at this period was subsequently matured by a study of the general interests of the Indian Empire, and the life of this virtuous nobleman terminated at a moment when his services, from the high station he had attained of President of the Board of Control, were most valuable to his country

[2] "This officer has been dead upwards of fifteen years

volunteer for Manilla, they only requested to know whether Colonel Oram would go with them: the answer was, 'He would.' 'Will he stay with us?' was the second question: the reply was in the affirmative, the whole corps exclaimed 'To Europe! to Europe!' and the alacrity and spirit with which they subsequently embarked, showed they would as readily have gone to the shores of the Atlantic as to an island of the eastern ocean Not a man of the corps deserted from the period they volunteered for service till they embarked; and such was the contagion of their enthusiasm that several Sepoys who were missing from one of the battalions in garrison at Madras were found, when the expedition returned, to have deserted to join the Twenty-second under Colonel Oram. We state this anecdote with a full impression of the importance of the lesson it conveys It is through their affections alone that such a class of men can be well commanded

"We meet in the Madras Native Army with many instances of unconquerable attachment to the service to which they belong Among these none can be more remarkable than that of Syud Ibrahim, commandant of the Tanjore cavalry, who was made prisoner by Tippoo Sultan in 1781 The character of this distinguished officer was well known to his enemy, and the highest rank and station were offered to tempt him to enter into the employment of the

State of Mysore. His steady refusal occasioned his being treated with such rigour, and was attended, as his fellow-prisoners (who were British officers) thought, with such danger to his life, that they, from a generous feeling, contemplating his condition as a Mahomedan and a native of India, as in some essential points different from their own, recommended him to accept the offers of the Sultan, but the firm allegiance of Syud Ibrahim would admit of no compromise, and he treated every overture as an insult His virtuous resolution provoked at last the resentment of Tippoo, and when the English prisoners were released in 1784, the commandant was removed to a dungeon in the mountain fortress of Couley Droog, where he terminated his existence. His sister, who had left her home, the Carnatic, to share the captivity of her brother, was subsequently wounded in the storming of Seringapatam. She, however, fortunately recovered, and the Government of Fort St George granted her a pension of fifty-two pagodas and a half per month, or £250 per annum, being the full pay of a native commandant of cavalry. A tomb was also erected at the place where Syud Ibrahim died, and Government endowed it with an establishment sufficient to maintain a fakeer or priest, and to keep two lamps continually burning at the shrine of this faithful soldier.

"Among the many instances of the effect which pride in themselves, and the notice of their superiors, inspire in this class of troops, we may state the conduct of the first battalion of the Eighth Regiment of infantry, which became, at the commencement of his career in India, a favourite corps[1] of the Duke of Wellington. They were with him on every service, and the men of this corps used often to call themselves 'Wellesley ka Pulten,' or Wellesley's Battalion, and their conduct on every occasion was calculated to support the proud title they had assumed. A staff officer,[2] after the battle of Assaye, saw a number of the Mahomedans of this battalion assembled apparently for a funeral. He asked whom they were about to inter? They mentioned the names of five commissioned and non-commissioned officers of a very distinguished family in the corps. 'We are going to put these brothers[3] into one grave,' said one of the party The officer, who was well acquainted with the individuals who had been slain, expressed his regret, and was about to offer some consolation to the sur-

[1] "This corps, some years before the period of which we are now speaking, attained very high reputation under Captain Dunwoody, an officer whose memory continues to be respected and cherished in the native army of Fort St George

[2] "The respectable and distinguished officer to whom we owe this and the following anecdote of the Madras troops, concludes a note he has been kind enough to send us on the subject with the following remark.—

"'I have seen,' he observes, 'the Madras Sepoys engaged in great and trifling actions more than fifty times I never knew them behave ill, or backward, but once, when two havildars (or serjeants) that were next to me quitted their post from seeing the fire chiefly directed at me, but it is,' he adds, 'but justice to state that, on other occasions, I have owed my life to the gallantry of my covering havildar'

[3] "The term 'brothers' extends in India to first cousins

vivors, but he was stopped by one of the men: 'There is no occasion,' he said, 'for such feelings or expressions. These men,' pointing to the dead bodies, 'were Sepoys (soldiers), they have died in the performance of their duty. The government they served will protect their children, who will soon fill the ranks they lately occupied.'

"Though sensible we have dwelt too long upon this part of our subject, we cannot forbear recording an example of that patience with which the native troops meet privation and distress. In 1804 the subsidiary force in the Deckan, commanded by Colonel Haliburton, was enclosed between two rivers, which became suddenly so swollen as to cut off their supplies of provisions. It was a period of general famine, and the communication was cut off with the grain-dealers, from whom alone they could expect a supply. All the rice in camp was found to be barely sufficient for five days' allowance, at a very reduced rate, to the European part of the force. Issues to the Sepoys were stopped; but while they were left to the scanty subsistence they might be able to procure for themselves, they were appointed the sole guards over that grain, from all share in which they were from necessity excluded. This duty was performed with the strictest care, and the most cheerful submission Fortunately the waters subsided, and an ample supply prevented their feeling that extreme of famine, the prospect of which they had contemplated with an attention to discipline, and a composure of mind which even astonished those best acquainted with their habits of order and obedience.

"We have before stated that it was at Bombay that the first native corps were disciplined by the English. Of the exact date we are ignorant, but regular Sepoys are noticed in the account of the transactions of that part of India some time before they were embodied at either Madras or Bengal. A corps of one hundred Sepoys from Bombay, and four hundred from Tellicherry, is mentioned as having joined the army at Madras in A D. 1747; and a company of Bombay Sepoys, which had gone with troops from Madras to Bengal, were present at the victory of Plassy. The Sepoys at Bombay continued long in independent companies, commanded by subadars or native captains. As the possessions and political relations of that settlement were enlarged, its army increased. The companies were formed into battalions under European officers, and during the war with the Mahrattas, A.D. 1780, we find the establishment consisting of fifteen battalions. These, at the termination of the war with Tippoo, 1783, were reduced to six, and one battalion of marines. In 1788 its numbers were augmented to twelve battalions. In 1796 it was reformed into an establishment of four regiments of two battalions each, from which it has been progressively raised by the acquisition of territory and subsidiary alliances to its present establishment of nine regiments of native infantry of two battalions each, one battalion of marines, and a small corps of native cavalry

"The men of the native infantry of Bombay are of a standard very near that of Madras. The lowest size taken is five feet three inches, and the average is five feet five; but they are robust and hardy, and capable of enduring great fatigue upon very slender diet.

"This army has, from its origin to the present day, been indiscriminately composed of all classes—Mahomedans, Hindoos, Jews, and some few Christians. Among the Hindoos, those of the lowest tribes of Mahrattas, and the Purwarrie, Soortee, and Frost[1] sects, are much more numerous than the Rajpoots and higher castes. Jews have always been favourite soldiers in this army, and great numbers of them attain the rank of commissioned officers.[2] It is probably owing to the peculiar composition, and to the local situation of the territories in which they are employed, that the

[1] "The Purwarrie are generally from the southward of Bombay, the Frost and Soortees from the northward These are men of what is termed very low caste, being hardly above what are called Pariahs on the coast of Coromandel.

[2] "We write from a memorandum of an officer of rank and experience in the Bombay army He observes 'The Jews are clean, obedient, and good soldiers make excellent non-commissioned and commissioned officers until they arrive at an advanced age, when they often fall off and turn drunkards.'

Sepoys of Bombay have at all periods been found ready to embark on foreign service. They are, in fact, familiar to the sea, and only a small proportion of them are incommoded in a voyage by those privations to which others are subject from prejudices of caste. But this is only one of the merits of the Bombay native soldier he is patient, faithful, and brave, and attached in a remarkable degree to his European officers. There cannot be a class of men more cheerful under privation and difficulties, and though desertion is very frequent among the recruits of this army, who, from the local position of Bombay, can on the first feeling of disgust at discipline, always in a few hours escape to the Mahratta territories, where they are safe from pursuit, there are no men, after they become soldiers, more attached to their colours. We question, indeed, if any army can produce more extraordinary examples of attachment to the government it served and to its officers than that of Bombay

"Towards the close of the war with Tippoo, in 1782, the whole of the force under General Mathews were made prisoners The Sultan, sensible of the advantages he might derive from the accession of a body of well-disciplined men, made every effort that he thought could tempt the English Sepoys into his service, but in vain. He ordered them to work upon his fortifications, particularly Chitteldroog, which was very unhealthy, upon a sear (two pounds) of ruggy (a small grain like mustard-seed), and a pice (about a halfpenny), per day. On this pittance they were rigidly kept at hard labour through the day, and in close confinement at night, subject to the continued insults of their guards; but neither insults, oppression, nor sickness, could subdue their fidelity; and at the peace of 1783, 1500[1] of the natives of India, who had been made prisoners near the mountains of the coast of Malabar, marched a distance of 500 miles to Madras, to embark on a voyage of six or eight weeks to rejoin the army to which they belonged at Bombay. During the march from Mysore, the guards of the Sultan carefully separated those men whenever they encamped by a tank (a large reservoir), or some other supposed insurmountable obstacle, from the European prisoners, among whom were their officers. Not a night passed—we write from a paper of an officer of distinction who was a witness of what he states—that some of the Sepoys did not elude the vigilance of their guards by swimming across the tank, or by passing the sentries, that they might see their officers, to whom they brought such small sums as they had saved from their pittance, begging they would condescend to accept the little all they had to give. 'We can live upon anything,' they used to say, 'but you require mutton and beef.'

[1] "A considerable number of the Sepoys taken with General Mathews had, at the hazard of their lives, made their escape from the Sultan and reached Bombay through the Mahratta territories.

"To the service in Egypt, in 1800, the Bombay troops proceeded with the same alacrity as to every other, and neither the new disorders (to them) of the ophthalmia or plague, from both of which they suffered, abated in the least degree their ardour. It happened that this force and that from Bengal were too late to share in the fame which our arms acquired in Egypt, but we can hardly contemplate an event in any history more calculated to inspire reflection on the character of that transcendent power which our country had attained than the meeting of her European and Indian armies on the shores of the Mediterranean.

"During the progress of the war with France, subsequent to 1803, several parties of the marine battalions of Bombay Sepoys were captured on board of the Company's cruisers, and carried to the Isle of France, where they were treated in a manner that reflects no credit upon the local government of that island, which probably expected that the hardships they endured would make them give way to the temptations continually held out, and induce them to take service; but in this they were disappointed—not one of these men could be persuaded to enter into the employment of the enemies of Great Britain, and when the Isle of France was captured, they met with that notice which they had so well merited. The government of Bombay granted to every individual who survived his captivity a silver medal as a memorial of the sense which it entertained of his proved fidelity and attachment.

"From the documents in our possession many examples of individual heroism in the Bombay Sepoy might be given, but we shall content ourselves with two, which will show, in a very strong point of view, the nature of their attachment to their European officers.

"Four years ago, when Major Hull, the commanding officer of a battalion on the Bombay establishment, was proceeding along the banks of a ravine, with eight or ten men of his corps, to search for some lions which had been seen near the cantonment of Kaira, in Guzerat, a royal tiger suddenly sprang upon him. The ground gave way, and the tiger and Major Hull rolled together to the bottom of the ravine. Though this fall prevented the latter from being killed by the first assault, still his fate seemed certain, and those who know, from having witnessed it, the terror which the attack of this fierce animal inspires, can alone appreciate the character of that feeling which led every Sepoy who was with him to rush at once to his succour. The tiger fell under their bayonets, though not before it had wounded two of the assailants most desperately—one having lost his leg, and the other being so lacerated as to be rendered unfit for future service as a soldier. These wounds, however, were deemed trivial by those who sustained them, when they saw that the officer whom they loved had escaped unhurt from his perilous situation.

"The second example of this strong feeling of duty is still more remarkable, as it was not merely encountering danger, but a devotion to certain death We take our account of the transaction from a document[1] in which it was recorded at the period of its occurrence.

"In 1797, Captain Packenham, in His Majesty's ship *Resistance*, accompanied by some small vessels of war belonging to the Company, took possession of Copong, the chief Dutch settlement on the eastern Isle of Timor. Lieutenant Frost, of the Bombay marine, commander of the *Intrepid* cruiser, who was to be appointed governor of Copong, had taken a house on shore, where he expected Captain Packenham to meet the Dutch governor and make arrangements for the future administration of the place. The Malays had formed a plan by which it was settled that the moment Captain Packenham landed to attend this meeting, they were to rise and murder all the Englishmen on shore. Fortunately something occurred to induce Captain Packenham to defer his visit; but he sent his boat, and its reaching the beach was the signal for the commencement of the massacre. Nearly twenty persons were slain. A large party had

[1] "Madras papers, 27th September 1797

rushed to Lieutenant Frost's house. The head of his surgeon had been struck off, and his own destruction seemed inevitable, when two Sepoys of the Bombay marine battalion whom he had landed from his vessel, exclaimed to him. 'Save yourself by flight, we will fight and die,' at the same time opposing themselves to the fury of the assailants, and giving their commander time to escape to a boat The Sepoys, after a resistance as protracted as they could render it, were slain, and their heads exposed on pikes explained their fate to their lamenting companions on board the *Intrepid* Captain Packenham took prompt and ample vengeance of this treachery He opened a heavy fire upon the place, under which he landed an efficient force, which defeated the Malays, who fled after losing two hundred men

"The length into which we have been led in our account of the native armies of Madras and Bombay must, in some degree, limit our observations on that of Bengal; but that is of less consequence, as those who desire to have complete information on this part of the subject can have recourse to the work before us. We shall, therefore, not dwell on details connected with the progress of this army, from a few companies who landed with Lord Clive in 1756, to its present number, which is upwards of 60,000 effective native soldiers, commanded by about 1500[1] European officers,

[1] "This is independent of the officers of artillery and engineers, and of

but content ourselves with noticing those facts which appear best calculated to illustrate the disposition and character of the materials of which it is composed.

"The narrative of Captain Williams, though not perhaps altogether calculated to please the fastidious reader, is throughout simple and intelligible; and the authenticity of his facts is confirmed by the manner in which they are related. His plan evidently was to give the history of each corps from the period in which it was raised till its dissolution, or till it was formed into a regiment of the present establishment, but having been an actor in many of the scenes he describes, he is insensibly led into digressions, which, though sometimes tedious, the reader will generally pardon, from the curious and interesting matter they contain

"The first battalions raised in Bengal were ten companies of 100 men each, commanded by a captain, with one lieutenant, one ensign, and one or two serjeants. Each company had a standard of the same ground as the facings, with a different device (suited to its subadar, or native captain), of a sabre, a crescent, or a dagger. The Company's colours, with the Union in one corner, were carried by the grenadiers. The first battalions were known by the name of the captain by whom they were commanded, and though,

invalid corps In 1760, the whole of the European officers in the service of the Company in Bengal amounted to eighteen captains, twenty six lieutenants, and fifteen ensigns in 1764, nineteen corps received a numerical rank corresponding with the actual rank of their commandants at that period, this did not prevent them from continuing to be known under their former appellation, or from assuming the name of a favourite leader; and it is under these names (which Captain Williams has faithfully preserved) that he gives the history of some of the most distinguished corps in the service He commences with an account of the 15th battalion, which he informs us was raised at Calcutta in 1757, and called the Mathews, from the name of its first commander. This corps was with Colonel Ford in 1759, when that able officer, with 346 Europeans, and 1400 Sepoys, besieged and took by storm the strong fortress of Masulipatam, making prisoners a French garrison, who, both in Europeans and natives, were nearly double his numbers In this daring and arduous enterprise we are told by the historian of India that 'the Sepoys (who lost in killed and wounded on the storm 200 men) behaved with equal gallantry as the Europeans both in the real and false attacks.'[1] In 1763, in the wars with the Vizier of Oude, the 'Mathews,' which was with the force under the command of Major Adams, is stated, when the Company's European regiment was broken by cavalry, to have nobly supported His Majesty's 84th Regiment, whose courage restored the action Major

[1] "Orme's *History of India*, vol iii p 489

Adams died shortly afterwards, and a general mutiny of the whole force took place, in which the Sepoys at first joined, but were soon after reclaimed to their duty. Captain Williams at this part enters into a long digression respecting the events of the period. He gives an account of the battle of Buxar, which was fought in 1764, and in which all the native corps appear to have behaved well, though the action was chiefly gained by the courage and discipline of the European part of the force

"In 1782, the Mathews was one of three Bengal corps who mutinied, under an apprehension of being embarked for foreign service; and though the conduct of these corps[1] was remarkable for the total absence

[1] "We cannot refrain from giving the following account of this mutiny, which is written by an officer who witnessed it It is very characteristical of the Bengal Sepoys 'The mutiny,' this officer observes, 'excepting a general spirit of murmur and discontent, was confined to the single instance of refusing the service, and whilst in that state preventing the march of two companies which were ordered to protect stores, etc, preparing for the expedition The men were guilty of no violence of any description, and treated their officers with the usual respect The discipline of the corps was carried on as usual, and notwithstanding some of the native officers, and men who had acted the most conspicuous part, were confined in the quarter-guards of their respective regiments, no attempt was made to release them After a lapse of several weeks, a general court-martial was held, and two subadars, and one or two Sepoys, were sentenced to death by being blown away from the mouth of cannon The sentence was carried into execution in the presence of those troops which had mutinied, excepting one other regiment, which was at the station, without the smallest opposition, or even murmur, and the troops were marched round the spot of execution amidst the mangled remains of their fellow-soldiers, without any other apparent feeling than the horror which such a scene was calculated to excite, and pity for their fate'

"The intended service was given up, and the regiments which had mutinied were pardoned in General Orders, but on the return to the

of that spirit of general insubordination and disposition to outrage by which mutinies of soldiery are usually marked, they were in the ensuing year broken, and drafted into some other battalions. 'Thus fell the Mathews,' says Captain Williams, 'a corps more highly spoken of during the twenty-six years it existed, than any battalion in the service; and at this day,' he adds, 'if you meet any of the old fellows who once belonged to it, and ask them what corps they came from, they will erect their heads and say, "Mathews ka pultan," or Mathews' battalion'

"The present second battalion of the 12th Regiment appears, from Captain Williams's account, to have been raised some months before the Mathews He indeed calls it the first raised battalion. This corps was at the battle of Plassy It was named by the Sepoys the Lal Pultan, or the Red [1] Battalion, and afterwards Gallis,[2] from the name of one of its first captains It was associated with the Mathews in all its early service, particularly at Masulipatam, Gheretty, etc, but in 1764 it mutinied, on the pretext of some promises which were made to it having been broken Having no apparent object, it was easily reduced to

Bengal provinces of General Goddard's detachment, the officers and men of the regiments which had mutinied were drafted into those old battalions

[1] "Probably from its dress

[2] "The name of this officer (who is still alive) is Galliez The natives of India often corrupt English names in an extraordinary manner, Dalrymple is made into *Dalduffle*, Ochterlony, *Lonyoechter*, Littlejohn, *John Litton*, Sharp, *Surrup*, etc etc

obedience; but Major Munro (afterwards Sir Hector Munro), who then commanded the army, thought a severe example necessary, and twenty-eight of the most guilty were tried by a drum-head court-martial and sentenced to death. Eight of these were directed to be immediately blown away from the guns of the force then at Choprah. As they were on the point of executing the sentence, three grenadiers, who happened to be amongst them, stept forth and claimed the privilege of being blown away from the right hand guns 'They had always fought on the right,' they said, 'and they hoped they would be permitted to die at the post of honour.' Their request was granted, and they were the first executed. 'I am sure,' says Captain Williams, who then belonged to the Royal Marines employed in Bengal, and who was an eye-witness of this remarkable scene, 'that there was not a dry eye among the Marines, although they had been long accustomed to hard service, and two of them had actually been in the execution party which shot Admiral Byng in the year 1757.'

"This corps subsequently distinguished itself in 1776, at the battle of Korah It had been known originally as the first battalion. It was afterwards numbered the 9th, from the rank of its captain In a new arrangement of the army it was made the 16th, then the 17th. By the regulations of 1796, it has become the 2d of the 12th Regiment; and it has of late years, as we shall hereafter have occasion to mention, far outdone its former fame. But we have said enough to show the style and object of Captain Williams's Memoir; we now proceed to the second part, or supplement of that work.

"There is sufficient internal evidence to satisfy us that the author of this part of the volume is an officer of experience and talent in the army which he describes. He is evidently possessed of the fullest information, and treats the subject like one who has made it the study of his life The affection and admiration which he evinces in every page for the native soldiery of Bengal made us peruse his account with an impression that he was a partial narrator of their deeds, but it is no more than justice to state that we have not discovered an instance in which his warm, and we may add enthusiastic, feelings have betrayed his judgment, and we have found throughout that his accuracy hardly ever admits a fact that is not supported by official record

"Though this part of the work professes to give an account of events subsequent to 1796, the author takes a retrospective view of the changes in the numbers and formation of the Bengal native army, from the earliest date till the publication of the regulations of that year. He also brings under our view the most remarkable military operations of the latter years of the administration of Mr. Hastings, of whose character and genius he speaks in a strain of eulogium the justice of which we are not disposed to question. When the standards of Hyder Ally floated over the desolated fields of the Carnatic, which the inert rulers of Madras had left exposed at every point to invasion; when a league of Mahratta leaders brought combined disgrace and discomfiture on the immature efforts of the government of Bombay; when internal rebellion threatened the peace of Bengal, and the opposition and violence of his colleagues embarrassed and impeded all his measures, the mind of Hastings derived energy from misfortune and fire from collision, and no one, we are convinced, can dispassionately read the history of the period to which we allude, without being satisfied that, to his intimate knowledge of the interests of the government which he administered, to his perfect acquaintance with the characters of every class of the natives, and to his singular power of kindling the zeal and securing the affections of those he employed, we owe the preservation of the British power in India. Among the wisest and boldest of the measures he adopted at this moment of public emergency was the sending of two great detachments from the native army of Bengal to Bombay and Madras. A general account of both these is given in the work before us. We shall first notice that which is prior in date.

"At the commencement of the year 1778,' says our

author, 'the presidency of Bombay having been seriously embarrassed by the pressure of the Mahratta war which then prevailed, the governor-general felt the necessity for effectual succour, both in specie and troops, being afforded to that quarter of the Honourable Company's possessions, with as little delay as possible Supplies of the former had been, and would again be, sent by sea, in the course of a six weeks' or two months' voyage (as well as by bills through the native bankers of Benares), but no such resource presented itself with regard to troops. On this emergency, the comprehensive mind of Warren Hastings formed the resolution (on his own responsibility, when opposed, as it was understood, by a majority of his colleagues in the government) to order a compact yet efficient detachment of native troops from the Bengal army to march across the continent of India 'through the hostile and unknown regions from the banks of the Ganges to the western coast of India,' to create a division in the councils and operations of the enemy, and eventually to co-operate with the Bombay Government and forces in the prosecution of the war in which they were involved'

"This detachment, which was composed of six native battalions, a corps of native cavalry, and a proportion of artillery, all together amounting to 103 European officers, 6624 native troops, with 31,000 followers, including the bazar, carriers of baggage, servants of officers, and families of Sepoys, had to march upwards of 800 miles through countries where every obstacle and opposition were to be overcome. It has been well observed by an excellent military author,[1] that an army in India has the appearance of

[1] "Lieutenant-General Dirom

'a nation emigrating, guarded by its troops.' To the mere European it would appear that this immense proportion of followers must encumber instead of aiding the progress of a corps on a long march, but those better instructed in Indian warfare know that it is, generally speaking, the number of followers which gives efficiency to an army in the East, as every person with it contributes (if the machine be well managed) in some manner or other to its support. The composition of an Indian army, and the scene of its operations, are so different from anything that is known in other countries, that we cannot be surprised at the erroneous judgment which those unacquainted with the subject so often form They forget that every luxury which they impute to the European in India originates not in a habit of indulgences but in an endeavour to obtain relief from severe suffering; and that if an Indian officer carries as great a quantity of wine, or other articles, which custom has rendered necessary, as he can, it is because he has little prospect after once the campaign has commenced of ever receiving another supply The country in which he operates furnishes nothing, and the communication with European settlements is in general, from the enemy's superiority in light cavalry, cut off. If he has a large and commodious[1] tent, it is because

[1] "We are assured that the Duke of Wellington, when he commanded the army in the Deckan, in 1803, actually ordered a corps to remain in

he cannot, from the nature of the climate, exist in a small one, the heat often rising, even in the best tents of the camp, to 110° of Fahrenheit's thermometer. If when ill he is carried in a dooly or palanquin, it is because there are no hospitals, or even depots, to which he can be sent, and there are often no roads on which light-wheeled carriages can travel. But the European soldier will understand the essential difference which exists between field service in India and in Europe, when told that owing to regard for the prejudices of the natives, and other causes, the term 'billet' is unknown in the former country; and that the troops in India seldom derive support, and never shelter or accommodation, from the villages and towns of the country in which they operate.

"But to return from this digression to the detachment which was ordered to the relief of the settlement of Bombay. Its first rendezvous was Culpee, a town on the right bank of the Jumnah, near Cawnpore, whence it commenced its march on the 12th of June 1778. It reached Rajgurh, a town in Bundelcund, on the 17th August, where it halted so much longer than Mr. Hastings thought necessary that he removed Colonel Leslie, the commanding officer, and appointed Lieutenant-Colonel Goddard to that charge. Under

garrison, and refused to allow it to advance with his army, because the officers had neglected to furnish themselves with tents of sufficient texture and size His experience had taught him how essential such tents were to preserve their health and to enable them to do their duty

this active and enterprising officer it continued its route through Malwah and Candeish to Surat, presenting the extraordinary spectacle of a corps of the natives of Hindostan, under the guidance of a few English officers, marching from the banks of the Ganges to the westernmost shores of India. During the five years that they were absent from their home, the men of this detachment conducted themselves in the most exemplary manner, and acquired distinction in every service in which they were employed. We shall not repeat the warm and animated eulogium which Mr. Hastings passed upon this corps in one of the last General Orders he issued to the army in Bengal, but we sincerely subscribe to the truth of his observation, that their conduct showed 'that there are no difficulties which the true spirit of military enterprise is not capable of surmounting.'

"The force despatched to the Carnatic in 1781 was commanded by Colonel Pearse. It consisted of five regiments of two small battalions (500 men each) of native infantry, some native cavalry, and a proportion of artillery. This corps, which marched about 1100 miles along the sea-coast, through the province of Cuttack and the Northern Circars to Madras, arrived at that presidency at a most eventful period, and their services were eminently useful to the preservation of our power in that quarter. Among the many occasions which this detachment had of distinguishing itself, the attack on the French lines at Cuddalore, in 1783, was the most remarkable. The Bengal Sepoys that were engaged on that occasion behaved nobly. It was, we believe, one of the first times that European troops and the disciplined natives of India had met at the bayonet The high spirit and bodily vigour of the rajpoots of the provinces of Bahar and Benares (the class of which three-fourths of this army was then composed) proved fully equal to the contest. In a partial action, which took place in a sortie made by the French, they were defeated with severe loss; and the memory of this event continues to be cherished with just pride both by the officers and men of the Bengal Native Army. Had the result of this affair, and the character of these Sepoys been more generally known, some of our countrymen would have been freed from that excessive alarm which was entertained for the safety of our Eastern possessions when the late despot of continental Europe threatened them with invasion. We trust that every event that can seriously disturb the peace of our Indian Empire is at a great distance; but if we even heard that an European army had crossed the Indus, we should not tremble for its fate. We well know that the approach of such a force would strike no terror into the minds of the men of whom we are writing, and that, acting with British troops, and led by British officers, they would advance with almost as assured a confidence of victory against a line of well-disciplined Europeans as against a rabble of their own untrained countrymen. They might fail; but they are too bold and too conscious of their own courage and strength ever to anticipate defeat.

"We should feel hesitation in stating our sentiments so strongly on this subject, if we did not know them to be those which have been entertained and avowed by many eminent commanders,[1] who have had opportunities of forming a judgment upon this question. When Colonel Pearse's detachment, which had been reduced by service from 5000 to 2000 men, returned to Bengal after an absence of four years, the policy of Mr Hastings heaped every distinction upon them that he thought calculated to reward their merits, or to stimulate others to future exertion of a similar nature. He visited this corps, and his personal conduct towards both the European officers and natives gave grace to his public measures A lasting impression[2] was made on the minds of all, and every favour was doubled by the manner in which it was conferred.

[1] "We may particularly quote the late Lord Lake No officer ever saw troops under more varied and severe trials than he did the Bengal Sepoys He never spoke of them but with admiration, and was forward to declare that he considered them equal to a contest with any troops that could be brought against them.

[2] "An officer of rank and distinction, who, when a young subaltern, was an eye-witness of this scene, observes in a letter which he has written to us on the subject 'Mr Hastings, dressed in a plain blue coat, with his head uncovered, rode along the ranks The troops had the most striking appearance of hardy veterans They were all as black as ink, contrasted with the sleek, olive skins of our home corps The sight of that day,' he concludes, 'and the feelings it excited, have never been

"The rebellion of Cheyt Singh, the Rajah of Benares, in 1781, must be familiar to most of our readers. Our purpose in mentioning it is limited to the object of showing the conduct of the Bengal Sepoys under one of the severest trials of fidelity to which they were ever exposed.

"The numerous followers of the Rajah had risen upon two companies of Sepoys appointed to guard the house in which he was placed under restraint, and killed and wounded the whole of them. The rashness of an European officer had led another party to slaughter in the streets of Ramnagur. Mr. Hastings, who was at Benares when these events occurred, had only a few companies of Sepoys to guard his person, and even these he had no money to support. He summoned corps from different quarters to his aid; but when we reflect on the impression which the first success of Cheyt Singh had made, and consider that by far the greatest proportion of the troops with whom Mr. Hastings had overcome the dangers with which he was surrounded were men of the same tribe and country as those against whom they were to act, and that the chief, who was declared a rebel, had long been considered by many of them as their legitimate prince, we must respect the mind that remained firm and unmoved at so alarming a crisis.

absent from my mind To it, and to the affecting orders (which Mr. Hastings issued) I am satisfied I in a great degree owe whatever of professional pride and emulation I have since possessed'

The knowledge Mr. Hastings had of the Sepoys, led him to place implicit trust in them on this trying occasion, and his confidence was well rewarded. Their habits of discipline and their attachment to their officers and the service, proved superior to the ties of caste and kindred Not an instance of defection occurred, and the public interests were preserved and restored by their zeal and valour.

"Before we make any remarks on the more recent parts of the history of the Bengal native infantry, we shall offer some observations on the composition of the army of that presidency. The native cavalry are not mentioned in the work before us, the authors having strictly adhered to the original intention of giving an account of the native infantry only. This corps, which now consists of eight regiments, is comparatively young. Its formation on the present establishment was only just completed when the Mahratta war of 1803 commenced. The conduct of the Bengal cavalry, however, in the severe service that ensued, has justly raised their reputation, and they at present form a most efficient and distinguished branch of the army to which they belong.[1] The men

[1] "We have only to peruse the despatches of the late Lord Lake, in 1803 and 1804, to be sensible of the excellence this corps very early obtained. We know few military exploits of cavalry more extraordinary than that which he performed with a column of three regiments of British light dragoons and three of native cavalry, supported by some horse artillery and a small reserve of infantry With this corps his lordship pursued Jeswunt Row Holkar from Delhi, through the Douab, till he came up with and defeated him at Futtyghur Lord Lake, in a despatch

are rather stouter than those in the same corps at Madras. The latter are almost all Mahomedans, and three-fourths of the Bengal cavalry are of the same race. The fact is, that with the exception of the Mahratta tribe, the Hindoos are not, generally speaking, so much disposed as Mahomedans to the duties of a trooper, and though the Mahomedans may be more dissipated and less moral in their private conduct than the Hindoos, they are zealous, and high-spirited soldiers, and it is excellent policy to have a considerable proportion of them in the service, to which experience has shown they often become warmly attached. In the native infantry of Bengal the Hindoos are in the full proportion of three-fourths to the Mahomedans They consist chiefly of Rajpoots, who are a distinguished race among the Khiteree or military tribe We may judge of the size of these men when we are told that the standard below which which no recruit is taken is five feet six inches[1] The great proportion of the grenadiers are six feet and upwards The Rajpoot is born a soldier. The mother speaks of nothing to her infant but deeds of arms,

dated 18th November, in which he gives an account of this operation, observes 'The troops have daily marched a distance of twenty-three or twenty-four miles During the night and day previous to the action, they marched fifty-eight miles, and from the distance to which they pursued the enemy, the space passed over before they had taken up their ground must have exceeded seventy miles'

[1] "Before 1796 it was always five feet six inches and a half By an order in 1809 men may be taken for light infantry corps as low as five feet five inches.

and every sentiment and action of the future man is marked by the first impressions that he has received If he tills the ground (which is the common occupation of this class), his sword and shield are placed near the furrow, and moved as his labour advances. The frame of the Rajpoot is almost always improved (even if his pursuits are those of civil life) by martial exercises He is from habit temperate in his diet, of a generous though warm temper, and of good moral conduct. He is, when well treated, obedient, zealous, and faithful Neither the Hindoo nor the Mahomedan soldier of India can be termed revengeful, though both are prone to extreme violence[1] in points where they deem their honour, of which they have a very nice sense, to be slighted or insulted. The Rajpoots sometimes want energy, but seldom, if ever, courage. It is remarkable in this class, that even when their animal spirits have been subdued so far as to cause a cessation of exertion, they show no fear of death,

[1] "One instance is given in the work before us of the action of this violent spirit In 1772 a Sepoy of the now first battalion of the 10th Regiment, who had suffered what he supposed an injury, fell out of the ranks when the corps was at exercise, and going up to Captain Ewens, the commanding officer, with recovered arms, as if to make some request, took a deliberate aim and shot him, then patiently awaited the death he had merited We could give, from our own knowledge, several examples of similar feeling Two will suffice Captain Crook, formerly of the Madras cavalry, struck a sentry for allowing a bullock that brought water to his tent to step over the threshold and dirty it The man took no notice of what had occurred till relieved from his post He then went to his lines, and a short time afterwards sought his captain, and taking deliberate aim at him, shot him dead upon the spot He made no attempt to escape He had avenged his bonour from the blows he had received,

series of actions and sieges, in every one of which the Bengal Sepoys showed their accustomed valour. At the battles of Delhi and Laswarree they were as eminently distinguished as at the sieges of Agra and Deeg; and we may, perhaps, safely assert that in the only two great reverses which occurred during the war, the retreat of Colonel Monson, and the siege of Burtpore, the courage, firmness, and attachment of the native troops were more conspicuous than in its most brilliant periods. We know sufficient of the former operations to regret that no full and faithful account of them has been yet published, nor does the work before us sufficiently supply this blank. We can only express our conviction, founded on a perusal of a private journal kept by an officer of the detachment, that in this disastrous retreat the native troops (with the exception of a very few, who, after suffering almost unparalleled hardships, were deluded by the offers of the enemy to desert) behaved in the most noble manner. They endured the greatest privations and distresses during the march from the banks of the Chumbul in Malwah, where the first retrograde movement was made, till their arrival at Agra, a distance of nearly 400 miles. They had at once to combat the elements (for it rained almost incessantly) and the enemy. Scenes of horror[1] occurred which were

[1] "Particularly at the Chumbullee Nullah, a rapid torrent, at which the elephants were employed to carry the troops over The animals, becoming wearied or impatient, shook off those on their backs, numbers

hardly ever surpassed. Yet, though deprived of regular food and rest, and harassed with continual attacks, their spirit was unbroken. They maintained throughout the most severe discipline. We are assured that on many occasions, when their European officers, worn down by the climate and fatigue, appeared faint or desponding, the men next them exclaimed, 'Keep up your heart, sir, we will take you in safety to Agra'[1] When in square, and sustaining charges from the enemy's horse, it more than once happened, when a musket was fired by a young soldier, that a veteran struck him with the butt-end of his firelock, exclaiming, 'Are you mad, to destroy our discipline and make us like the rabble that are attacking us?'

"The only serious impatience that the Sepoys of this detachment showed, was to be led against the enemy; and the manner in which they behaved on all occasions given them of signalizing their valour, showed that this feeling had its rise in no vain confidence. The flank companies, under Captain

of whom were drowned But a still more horrid scene ensued The fatigued elephants could not bring over the followers. The Bheels, a mountain banditti, encouraged by Holkar, came down upon the unprotected females and children, whom they massacred in the most inhuman manner. It was on this extreme trial that some of the gallant fellows, who had before suffered every hardship with firmness, gave way to despair Several of them, maddened with the screams of their wives and children, threw themselves, with their firelocks, into the rapid stream, and perished in a vain attempt to aid those they loved more than life

[1] "We have been informed of this fact by officers to whom these expressions were used

O'Donnell, were very successful in beating up the quarters of a considerable corps of the enemy on the 21st July. On the 24th of August, when all the detachment, which consisted of five battalions and six companies of Sepoys, had been sent across the Bannas river, except the 2d battalion of the 2d Regiment and some pickets, Holkar brought up his infantry and guns to attack this corps, which not only defended its position, but advanced with the utmost gallantry, and obtained possession of several pieces of the enemy's artillery. It could not, however, be supported by the other parts of the force, who were divided from it by the river, and it was almost annihilated. Those who witnessed the attack which it made upon Holkar's line from the opposite bank of the Bannas, speak with admiration of the heroism of the European officers, and of the gallant men whom they led to a momentary but fatal victory. At the close of this affair they saw a jemadar (native lieutenant) retiring towards the river, pursued by five or six men He held the standard of his battalion in one hand, and a sword, with which he defended himself, in the other. When arrived at the river he seemed to have attained his object of saving the colours of his corps, and, springing with them into the current, sunk to rise no more.

"There have been few officers who better understood the character of soldiers than the late Lord Lake. He had early discovered that of the Bengal

Sepoys. He attended to their prejudices, flattered their pride, and praised their valour. They repaid his consideration of them with gratitude and affection, and during the whole of the late Mahratta war, their zeal and devotion to the public service was increased by the regard and attachment which they entertained for the Commander-in-chief. Sufficient instances of this occur in the work now before us. There is none, however, more remarkable than the conduct he pursued towards the shattered corps of Colonel Monson's detachment. He formed them into a reserve, and promised them every opportunity of signalizing themselves. No confidence was ever better repaid, and throughout the service that ensued these corps were uniformly distinguished

"The conduct of the 2d battalion of the 12th Regiment may be taken as an example of the spirit that animated the whole. This corps, which has been before noticed under its first name of 'Gillhez,' or the the Lal Pultan, had behaved with uncommon valour at the battle of Laswarree, where it had 100 men and 3 officers killed and wounded. It was associated on that occasion with his Majesty's 76th Regiment, and shared in the praise which Lord Lake bestowed on 'the handful of heroes,' as he emphatically termed those whose great exertions decided that battle. It was with Colonel Monson's detachment, and maintained its high character in the disastrous defeat we have alluded to. But all its former deeds were outdone at the siege of Burtpore. It appears by a printed memorial which we have before us of its European commanding officer, that on the first storm of that fortress this corps lost 150 officers and men killed and wounded, and did not retire till the last. On the third attack, when joined with the 1st battalion of the same regiment (amounting together to 800 men), it became the admiration of the whole army. The 2d battalion of the 12th Regiment on this occasion not only drove back the enemy who had made a sally to attack the trenches, but effected a lodgment, and planted its colours on one of the bastions of the fort. Unfortunately this work was cut off by a deep ditch from the body of the place, and after the attack had failed, the 12th Regiment was ordered to retire, which they did reluctantly, with the loss of 7 officers and 350 men killed and wounded, being nearly half the number they had carried into action.

"Examples of equal valour might be given from any other corps during the war, and instances of individual valour might be noticed in any number, but more is not necessary to satisfy the reader of the just title of the Bengal Sepoys to the high name which they have acquired, and from late accounts[1] we per-

[1] "We know few instances where more has been required from the zeal and valour of the native troops, than in the late campaign against the Goorkhas. The great successes of Major-General Sir D. Ochterlony could only have been gained by the patience and courage of the troops

ceive that their conduct throughout the arduous service in Nepaul, where they had at once to contend with the natural obstacles of an almost impracticable country, and the desperate valour of a race of hardy mountaineers, has been worthy of their former fame since the conclusion of this war a small body of these troops has had an opportunity of exhibiting, in a most distinguished manner, that firmness, courage, and attachment to their officers and the service, which have always characterized this army. We allude to a recent occurrence of a most serious sedition at Bareilly, the capital of Rohilcund. The introduction of a police tax, intended to provide means for the security of life and property, had spread alarm and discontent among an ignorant population, whose prejudices in favour of their ancient usages are so strong as to lead them to regard any innovation (whatever be its character) with jealousy and indignation Acting under these feelings, the Rohillas of Bareilly, who are alike remarkable for their strength of body

being equal to the skill and decision of their commander, and in the spirited and able operations of Colonel Nicolls, quarter-master-general of his Majesty's troops in India, against Almorah, where 800 Sepoys, aided by a few irregulars, were led against 3000 gallant mountaineers, who occupied that mountain fortress and the heights by which it was surrounded Victory could only have been obtained by every Sepoy partaking of the ardour and resolution of his gallant leader. Of their conduct on this occasion we may, indeed, judge by the admiration with which it inspired Colonel Nicolls, who gave vent to his feelings in an order that does honour to his character Speaking of an attack made by a party of Sepoy grenadiers, he observes, 'This was an exploit of which the best troops of any age might justly have been proud.'

and individual courage, rose in a body to oppose the orders of the civil magistrate. They were led by a priest upwards of ninety years of age, who dug his grave to indicate his resolution to conquer or die, and at whose orders the green flag, or standard of Mahomet, was hoisted, that religious feelings might be excited to aid the efforts which they now proclaimed themselves determined to make to effect the downfall of their European tyrants. What rendered this revolt more alarming was the knowledge that the cause of the insurgents was popular over the whole country, and a belief that their success would be the signal for a general rise in the neighbouring provinces. All the force that could be collected to suppress this revolt was a detachment of between three and four hundred Sepoys of the 27th Regiment of native infantry, and part of a provincial battalion under Captain Boscawen, with two guns and a party of about 400 Rohilla horse belonging to a corps lately embodied under Captain Cunningham. The former received, with undismayed courage, the charge of an undisciplined, but furious and desperate rabble, who, encouraged by their numbers, which exceeded 12,000 armed men, persevered in the attack till more than 2000 of them were slain; and the latter, though of the same class and religion as the insurgents, and probably related to many of them by the ties of kindred, proved equally firm as the Sepoys to their duty. When their priest advanced and invoked them to join their natural friends, and to range themselves under the standard of their faith, only one man was found wanting in fidelity; he deserted, and was soon afterwards slain by his former comrades, who continued throughout to display prompt obedience, exemplary courage, and unshaken attachment to the officer by whom they were led.

"However slight this affair may seem, we do not recollect any occurrence in the history of British India more calculated to show the dependence of our power on the fidelity of our native troops, and the absolute necessity of adopting every measure by which their attachment can be confirmed and approved. We are as jealous as Englishmen ought to be, of the encroachment of military power, whenever we meet the pretensions or privileges of soldiers marshalled in opposition to the rights of the civil part of the community. The whole bias of our minds is to support the latter; but it is not the part of wisdom to transplant the feelings, the principles, and the maxims, that are essential to the maintenance of the constitution of our native country to India. The soil is not yet prepared for their reception, and it probably never will be. It is, no doubt, our duty to make our government as mild, as just, and as equal in its benefits to every class of our subjects, as it is possible, consistent with attention to the general security; but we must not make ourselves the slaves of our own rules. If we are told, which it is not improbable we may be, that this doctrine has a tendency to infringe some of the most essential of our civil regulations, we must answer that we know of no principle or institution in a government which ought not to yield to another that can be proved necessary for the preservation of the State; and that we must have stronger instances than the history of India yet affords, of the power of our civil regulations and establishments to save us from danger, before we can be convinced that they should not be altered and remodelled, in any points, when alteration would decidedly furnish us with additional means of permanently rewarding and preserving the courage and attachment of that class of the natives of India, to whom we are, by our condition, compelled to confide the sword for the defence and protection of our empire in that quarter of the globe.

"We have in the work before us several accounts of mutinies among the Bengal Sepoys, but these appear, in almost all cases, to have proceeded from one of two causes: the nefarious or unjustifiable conduct of the commander of the corps, or an attempt to make them proceed by sea on foreign service. The former cause of discontent is not so likely to occur under the present regulation as it was at a period when the command of a battalion could be converted into a source of indirect emolument; and the latter will be avoided as long as the present system continues of forming volunteer[1] battalions for expeditions that require embarkation.

"We shall conclude our observations upon the Bengal Sepoys with two quotations from the Supplement of Captain Williams's Memoir, which we give, first, as a fair specimen of the style and feeling in which this part of the work is written, and secondly, as memorable examples of what the European officers, who understand this class, can effect, and how possible it is to bring them to the highest state of discipline and yet preserve to the fullest degree their temper and attachment.

"'Proceeding from Culpee,' the author observes, when speaking of the force under Colonel Goddard, 'the detachment lost on the second day's march one of its most valuable officers, Captain James Crawford, commanding the fourth battalion, who died from a stroke of the sun. Connected with this unfortunate event, the following facts will doubtless be read with unfeigned sympathy and admiration Captain Crawford had acquired the character of an excellent

[1] "It has been found by experience, that though, from causes before mentioned, corps, collectively, are usually unwilling to embark, volunteers for this species of service can be obtained to any amount The young men who enter these temporary corps with the hopes of distinction and promotion are perhaps the best suited to the service The number and quality of the native troops who volunteered from Bengal for the wars of 1791-2 and 1799, in Mysore, in 1810, for Egypt, and in 1810 and 1811, for the Isles of France and Batavia, may be adduced as complete proofs of the truth of this assertion. It formed a part of the able administration of the Marquis Wellesley to conciliate and attach the native troops by every possible means, and his attention was particularly and successfully directed to encourage them to volunteer for the foreign service Lord Minto adopted similar measures with equal success

Sepoy officer, and the battalion which he commanded was considered as one of the finest in the service The appellation of "Crawford," by which the fourth battalion was called by the men of the corps and the natives in general, was an exception to the practice that generally prevailed in former times, of calling corps by the name of the officer by whom they were formed, or that of the place at which they were raised.

"'Captain Crawford was considered by the men as a rigid, and, perhaps, severe disciplinarian, yet that excellent officer so happily blended with the strictest principles of military discipline and arrangement the practice of the most inflexible integrity and impartial justice, in the general exercise of the influence and powers of authority, combined with considerate and manly indulgence in regard to the religious habits, the customs and prejudices of the men under his command, that of Captain Crawford it may with truth be affirmed, he had the peculiar good fortune of verifying what ought to be the object and emulation of every military man, with regard to those under his command, the enviable distinction of commanding their lives through the medium of their affections It is a fact no less creditable to Captain Crawford's memory than it is honourable to the character of the men whom he commanded, that during the halt of the detachment at the encampment where he was interred (which continued for several days, owing to the severity of the weather), all the corps, native officers and men, went from time to time to render their tribute of grateful attachment and affection, by making their obeisance, after the manner of their country, at the grave of their lamented commander, and on the day that the detachment moved forward from that encampment, the grateful and sorrowing "Crawford," after the battalion had been told off preparatory to the march, requested leave to pile their arms and be permitted, collectively, to go and express their last benedictory farewell over the remains of their respected commander, protector, and friend What soldier,' our author emphatically concludes, 'can read this without exclaiming, May my last end be like his!'

"The second proof which our author gives of the attachment of the native troops of Bengal force to their commanding officer, when his character is worthy of it, refers to an event nearly forty years subsequent, and we rejoice to see that time has made no alteration in the character of feelings that are honourable not only to those by whom they are entertained, but to human nature

"'Meritorious and indefatigable as were the exertions of all the officers who were employed in raising and forming the new corps (24th, 25th, 26th, and 27th), it will be no disparagement to them to declare that the 2d battalion of the 25th, under Captain Christie, surpassed the others by its more early appearance of military efficiency and perfection

"'Captain Christie was blessed with that happy beneficence of disposition which made it his constant practice and delight to blend paternal kindness and conciliation with the requisite authority as an officer To use the words of an eye-witness, Captain Christie had raised, clothed, and disciplined the corps with all the tenderness of a parent, and the pride and solicitude of a soldier, the commander and the men were proud of each other But he had barely accomplished this first wish of his heart, in bringing the corps to maturity, when he was seized with a violent illness, which in a few days deprived the corps and the service of a valuable and exemplary officer

"'Captain Christie died on the 30th of April 1805, and was buried at Saintree, on the left bank of the Jumna, between Agra and Muttra. The native officers of the corps, so contrary to their customs and religious prejudices, solicited permission to carry the corpse of their beloved commander to the grave The whole corps followed the mournful procession with a general countenance of affliction and grief, presenting one of the most affecting scenes I ever beheld. After the funeral ceremony, each Sepoy stepped forward to look into the grave, threw a clod of earth on the coffin, and retired in melancholy silence, the whole corps sorrowing in tears'[1]

"The novelty and interest of this subject have seduced us far beyond those limits which we had prescribed to ourselves in treating it; and we must therefore pass over those observations which we purposed to make regarding the means best calculated to secure the continuance of the attachment of our native troops to their officers and to the service. This is, however, of less consequence, as the lesson is already conveyed through the facts which we have stated It

[1] "Further examples of this feeling are given in the work before us, and we could, from our own knowledge, adduce several proofs of similar attachment in the Sepoys of the other establishments One will suffice Major Thomas Little, of the Madras native infantry, whose great kindness and mildness of manners were only equalled by his firmness and thorough knowledge of his duties as an officer, died last year, when the army was encamped in the ceded districts His corps, a battalion of light infantry, had been reviewed a few days before his death, and was pronounced by the commander-in-chief, Sir T Hislop, to be in the highest state of discipline, yet so well had this admirable Sepoy officer (we choose the term as denoting peculiar duties) preserved the temper of his men, that not satisfied with mourning him they requested leave to erect a tomb to his memory

is by treating the Sepoys with kindness and consideration, by stimulating their pride, and by attending, in the most minute manner, to their feelings and prejudices, that we can command, as has been well observed, 'their lives through the medium of their affections;' and so long as we can, by these means, preserve the fidelity and attachment of that proportion of the population of our immense possessions in the East, which we arm to defend the remainder, our empire may be considered as secure.'"

Note.—My most sincere thanks are due to Mr. Murray for allowing me to reproduce the above from the *Quarterly Review* of 1817, which throws so much light on the nature of the Indian army.—A. MACLEOD.

III

THE IRREGULAR FORCES OF INDIA.

As the foregoing gives so admirable an account of the *Regular* native armies of the three Presidencies, I shall now give an account of the *Irregular* (or Sillahdar) forces of India This account is my own Report of the Mysore Sillahdars in the year 1844. And as the Sillahdars of all India are pretty much alike, this account may give a fair idea of how they are raised and maintained, and of their importance in times of war and their usefulness in time of peace [1]

I lay this account in all its details before the public, as the safety and preservation of India will likely ever depend more upon the efficient maintenance of irregulars than upon the maintenance of a large standing army. I do not mean that we can dis-

[1] Their usefulness in times of peace may be very briefly explained Shortly after the inspection of the Sillahdars (Mysore cavalry) by General Lovell, in 1841, they were, by order of the Commissioner, broken up into many small detachments to assist the civil authorities, and although their being thus partially removed from the immediate control of their own superior officers could not but in some degree relax their discipline, as became apparent when they were reassembled in regiments, yet I viewed their falling off in this respect as not very important, while in *esprit de corps* and fidelity to the Government they happily remained unshaken This estimate of the Sillahdars, serving in this capacity, is confirmed in letters to come before the reader in the sequel

pense with a standing army; but from the nature of the country and its people, without the loyal and hearty co-operation of these irregulars, the preservation of India from foreign aggression is of the utmost uncertainty, but with a numerically small standing army, and a loyal and well-disciplined irregular force on the Sillahdar system, we can bid defiance to the world.

There are two very obvious objections to a standing army alone for the preservation of India. The one is that the fate of India would depend upon the issue of a battle or battles; and the other is that the maintenance of an army sufficiently great would entail too great a drain upon the physical and material resources of our country.

By the maintenance of an efficient irregular force, it is not only absolute security that is guaranteed, but on this system there would be immunity from extraneous expenditure; for the system upon which the Sillahdar is upheld, is that the natives are defending themselves and their country, and that too at their own expense. Every rupee of their pay is as regularly spent in the country as it is issued to these officers and men, and the greater part, if not almost the whole, is in the form of land revenue, repaid into the Circar Treasury within the year. Such I and my native officials believed was the fact when I had charge of the Nuggur Division, and it doubtless will ever be the same.

Moreover, the system of irregular warfare is intuitive to the natives of India, and so complete and perfect is their knowledge of this system, when they are not divided among themselves, and have a common cause, however much they may be inferior to disciplined aggressive forces, that their adroitness and negative resources of exhausting an enemy are almost matchless and incredible, as may be seen in the following report, in the instance of Lord Cornwallis and the Mahrattas[1]

Supposing that India is any day attacked by a foreign foe, and is met by our regular force, what would it avail the enemy although our army was beat in one, two, or a dozen battles, when these Sillahdars can so effectually strip a country as to make it a desert, can so exactly apprise of an enemy's every movement and position, and, by a system of unceasing and effectual harassing, literally exterminate any aggressive army in the world that would be foolhardy enough to enter into the country? Indeed, they are not able to do this last of themselves; but with a comparatively small regular British army, or at least with a well organized and equipped army under British officers, if they are true to themselves and their own interest, and at one with England, they may congratulate themselves upon being the most secure country in the world against any foreign aggression for generations to come

[1] See pages 135 and 136

For these reasons I make no further apology in giving a detailed account of so important an auxiliary to our military force in India; and though it may not all be interesting to the general reader, it may give information to all who, from position or occupation, are deeply interested in the well-being of India, and may also serve as a complement to the foregoing able account of the regular forces, and thus, as it were, furnish the reader with a complete idea of the native forces of India, and what is of more importance, it will convince any native who may read it, that the disposition and intentions of Britain towards India are the very best, and that the only safety of himself, his family, and of India, is to be at one with Britain in loyalty and obedience to our common Queen and Government.

No. 224.

To the Secretary to the Commissioner for the Government of the Territories of the Rajah of Mysore.

SIR,

1. I have the honour to request you will submit to the Commissioner the following observations on the Sillahdar Horse, which in nature and constitution differ so widely from our regular troops, that it is impossible to lay down fixed rules for their discipline and management. I should long since have complied

with the orders of the Commissioner on this subject, but that I was anxious to furnish a report which should explain the interior economy and entire arrangements of every regiment separately, so that he might judge of the state of each, as easily as is done by reading the review report on one of our own cavalry regiments. After many attempts, I found that any report made out with this view would not give so clear an idea of the whole system as a general statement of the manner in which my duties as military assistant are conducted without the intervention of Buckshees, I however trust that the following pages will give all the information required by your letters noted in the margin,[1] and that my future annual reports will keep the Commissioner fully informed on all points relating to the Sillahdars.

2. *Office of Buckshee*.—Notwithstanding the corrupt practices of the Buckshees, which led to their suspension from office, a remarkable improvement was effected in the Mysore Sillahdars, between the inspection made by Lieutenant-Colonel Conway in 1833, and my first inspection in 1840. Lieutenant-Colonel Conway, in his report dated 22d April 1833, describes the Sillahdars as "ill mounted, badly dressed, not armed as soldiers, destitute of appointments, inferior men, with unsoldierlike habits, and deficient in

[1] 3d February 1840, No 56, 15th September 1841, No 459, 30th May 1842, No 33, 10th May 1844, No 241

discipline." They were in 1840 no longer deserving of such censure, all the men and horses improperly introduced having been got rid of, and a better system of internal management introduced. The Sillahdars have always borne the character of fidelity to the Government they serve, and freely admitting the corrupt practices of their former Buckshees, are now decidedly in favour of direct European superintendence. It is true that several natives of rank have advocated the restoration of the appointment, but they were all men who considered themselves eligible for it. The Regimentdars were individually candidates, but it is well known that any one of them, if not himself made Buckshee, would prefer being under the direct superintendence of the European officer Under these, and other circumstances which have come to my notice, but which it would be superfluous to mention in a report, it is my decided opinion that the military assistant should continue to exert, as at present, a direct supervision over the whole establishment

3. *Inspections, and issue of Pay.*—On making my first inspection of the seven regiments in 1840, I compared every man and horse with the registers, and questioned separately every officer and Sillahdar as to whether he had any complaints to make, and whether he regularly received his pay, none made any complaint worthy of notice, and all replied that they had regularly received their whole pay ever since

the Buckshees had been suspended from office. On this point I continue to bestow much attention, taking every private opportunity of questioning the men as to their pay, besides continuing to do so at all inspections. Since the appointment of military assistant, pay has been issued to the Sillahdars as punctually as to our regular troops; but Sillahdars are kept one full month in arrears, *i e* pay for January is issued in March. As little fraud or extortion is now committed in the Sillahdar establishment as in any establishment in India.

4. *Old Sillahdars may resign in favour of their Sons.*—Remarking a great number of very old men in the first regiment inspected, I asked them why they did not resign in favour of their sons, and found that although their exchanging had been always authorized by the Government (both native and European), yet their Buckshees had managed to keep them in ignorance on the subject, and generally exacted a large fee before granting the indulgence. All such fees have of course been done away with, and the free privilege is considered a great boon, while, by its introducing young men into the service, the efficiency and appearance of the Sillahdars is improved.

5. *Barrgheers registered as Sillahdars*—At the same inspection, on my observing to the officers that some of their men did not answer to their registered names, they explained that an order abolishing Barr-

gheers had led to many instances of false registering, and that several men registered as Sillahdars were but Barrgheers.[1] Although these men had, strictly speaking, forfeited their situations, yet, as they could not be at once discharged without causing general discontent, I called upon the Regimentdars to furnish a list of all such men in their respective regiments, promising that none who then declared his actual position should be discharged. By these lists it appeared that 179 Barrgheers were falsely registered as Sillahdars The horses of 63 of these had been left by deceased Sillahdars to sons or near relations, who have since grown up, and taken the place of their Barrgheers, in 90 other instances arrangements have been made between

[1] A Sillahdar is a man whose registered horse is actually his own property A Barrgheer Sillahdar keeps, feeds, rides the horse, and draws the full pay from Government, but makes over a portion of it to the rightful owner of the horse Many of the officers are allowed to keep a limited number of Barrgheers, which of course are registered as such In the event of our disbanded regiments of Light Cavalry being raised as Sillahdars, I certainly think it would be most desirable openly to sanction this Barrgheer system to a large extent Few of our former native officers and troopers would have funds of their own to purchase good chargers, but an owner's allowance out of a Sillahdar's pay would be a safe and lucrative investment This would induce rich natives or even Indian banks to purchase the chargers, especially fine brood mares, were breeding allowed, which it certainly ought to be, as it was in the time when I was military assistant I would here observe that the system of breeding was objectionable, which only lately I was reminded of, by a perusal of the Blue Book published by the India Council I observed on perusing it that breeding in India was less successful than, I think, it ought to be When I was in India, in the hope of doing good, I then forwarded a "Memorandum on Breeding" (which I prepared at Bangalore) to Sir Mark Cubbon, but which was rejected, as we of the Mysore Commission had "nothing to do with breeding," which was under the Madras Commissariot I lately sent my memorandum to Major John Campbell, secretary of the Mysore Commission, but of course not officially

the owners and Barrgheers, so that the number of these Barrgheers registered as Sillahdars is reduced to 26.

6. *Enlisting of Sillahdars.*—The above discovery proving the necessity of some security against imposition when replacing Sillahdars, I ordered that every candidate for a Sillahdaree, when sent for examination previous to filling up a vacancy, should bring a certificate, stating in full his claims for employment, which certificate is signed by the Ressaldar of the Ressallah in which the vacancy takes place, and countersigned by the Regimentdar, in token of their responsibility for its correctness. This arrangement prevents officers from passing over the families of deserving old Sillahdars,—for not a man in the service dies that the Regimentdar does not report whether he has or has not left a relation fit to succeed him But to guard against impositions likely to be practised by the owner of a horse, when the candidate is intended to replace a worn-out or deceased Sillahdar, a deed, making over the horse to him from the former owner, or from the heir of the deceased (as the case may be), is also required. A great check has thus been put to the practice of clandestinely filling the ranks with Barrgheers, as it is very seldom that one native will so far trust another as to make over a horse to him, on his simple promise of paying so much a month out of his salary. When a near relation to a deceased Sillahdar appears before the military assis-

tant with the above vouchers, and the man is in all respects fit for the service, the recommendation he brings from the Regimentdar and Ressaldar is confirmed, but although it is only justice to these officers to say that they give these recommendations, whether for enlistments or for promotions, with great impartiality and discretion, it is proper to observe that, if without control, there is reason to fear that they would soon act unjustly, from partiality to their private friends, or for still less meritorious reasons The Buckshees of course had their own partialities, they even took the entire patronage of some regiments into their own hands, and I am disposed to believe that the confidence which the Regimentdars and Ressaldars consider to be placed in them, from having their recommendations so much attended to, contributes in no slight degree to the feeling which I have already mentioned as existing among them respecting the office of Buckshee The Sillahdars openly assert that they prefer the present arrangement, because they get their whole pay regularly, because when old and worn out, they are freely permitted to resign in favour of their sons, and because, when they die leaving sons or brothers fit for the service, their appointment to it insures a provision for their families. It need scarcely be remarked that nothing so much attaches a native to the Government which he serves, as finding that it shows care and consideration not only for its soldiers, but for their families also. When a Sillahdar dies without leaving behind him a relation with sufficient claims on the Government to call for his being appointed to the vacant Sillahdaree, the Regimentdar sends in the name of some young man he considers eligible, but such vacancies are usually filled by men selected by the military assistant, who keeps a list of candidates having well-grounded claims

7. *Promotions.*— Regimentdars send in to the military assistant recommendations for filling up all vacancies amongst their officers, and when the rank is above that of Jemadar, he submits the claims and merits of each individual to the consideration of the Commissioner, without whose previous sanction no promotion is given to any man who has not served upwards of three years as a Sillahdar, and the English monthly returns regularly afford to the Commissioner all information concerning the claims of each individual promoted or enlisted.

8. *Furlough.*—The following arrangements concerning leave are found to answer well, and to give general satisfaction. Regimentdars are authorized to grant leave of absence to ten men (officers included) per regiment for 15 days each within the monthly returns; each Ressaldar has the power of giving leave to five of his Ressallah, and each Jemadar to two of his Biradery—the former for six and the latter for three

days between those appointed for weekly exercise. All other applications for leave are made to the military assistant, and granted to the extent of 32 men (officers included) per regiment, mention being made in each instance whether the applicant has been on furlough within the two last years. Lest it should be considered that the Sillahdars are allowed an unusual proportion of leave, it may here be mentioned, that from Buckshees leave could be obtained by a greater number of men, and for a much longer period than at present, but few, excepting those who would pay well for it, received this indulgence, and the granting of it without payment is considered by the poor Sillahdar a great benefit If returned to his duty before his term of leave is expired, a man gets the whole arrears of his pay immediately, and a report of his having done so is sent to the military assistant, but to men overstaying their time no arrears are paid without previous reference to that officer, and unless a good and sufficient reason is given for such absence, not only the arrears are forfeited, but the man's leave of absence stopped for two years

9 *Horses.*—In no respect did the late military assistant, Major Hunter, effect a greater improvement than in the efficiency, condition, and appearance of the horses; and from his acknowledged excellent judgment of horses, no one could be better calculated to remedy the evils formerly existing in this depart-

ment. By Lieutenant-Colonel Conway's report, the Sillahdars, at the assumption of the country, were most indifferently mounted, while Major Hunter, in his report dated 6th August 1837, says that "their description of horse is excellent for their purpose, and although (generally speaking) of lower standard than the horses of the Madras cavalry, yet they are not inferior to them for the duties of irregular horse, exhibiting much blood, and being stout, active, and hardy," an opinion which is fully supported by the best judges, and the experience of the Sillahdars employed on duties of fatigue

10. *Breeding* —Since the date of Major Hunter's report 92 horses have been received on account of an increase to the establishment, and 1136 in place of others dead or unfit for the service Of these, 414 were bought from dealers, and 814 bred in Mysore The purchase of so many foreign horses was occasioned by the breeding from mares in the service having been stopped from October 1834 to January 1842, but breeding having been renewed to the extent of 1000 of the best mares, the necessity of Sillahdars getting horses of a foreign breed no longer exists, and as a Sillahdar, in case of his service being required, is bound to find a substitute should his mare be in foal, the trifling hindrance which the breeding may be to his progress in field-exercise is scarce worthy of notice compared with the advantage which the State will

derive from being able in a few years to remount the cavalry of this Presidency on horses bred in the country at less cost than imported ones, besides that of circulating in our own dominions the large capital thus expended, instead of its passing as formerly into the hands of Arabs, Persians, and other foreigners.

11. *Replacing of Horses*—It has long been a standing rule that on the death of a Sillahdar's horse he is allowed one month to provide another, without loss of his pay, and when a horse is killed, or incurably injured in action, or on a forced march, the owner is entitled to his registered price from Government But these just regulations were formerly much abused, and in most instances it was necessary for a Sillahdar to pay a considerable sum in order to prevent a fresh horse from being rejected. The present method is that the Regimentdar examines each horse brought by a Sillahdar as a substitute for another, and (giving his opinion as to its fitness) forwards it with the owner for the military assistant to examine, and register if approved of The circumstance of a Sillahdar not providing himself with a good horse when required is now unknown. The officers of all ranks take considerable pride in seeing their men well mounted, as indeed do the Sillahdars themselves, so that on my pointing out any horse unfit for the service no delay occurs in replacing it, except where arising from the owner's poverty, in which case, if

requested by his officer, a few months for procuring a substitute are invariably granted.

12 *Price of a Horse*—The average price paid by a Sillahdar for a horse or mare is about 325 rupees. It seldom happens that a Sillahdar has money enough to pay down at once for the animal, or this average would not be above 250 rupees. When one Sillahdar buys a horse from another on credit, at least 20 per cent. more is charged than if the price were paid down at once, and the whole sum is then defrayed by the customary instalments of 10 rupees a month. But when the horse is purchased from a dealer, the money is generally borrowed from a Sowar at the exorbitant interest of 24 per cent. per annum.

13. *Colts and Fillies how disposed of.*—Colts that give promise of being fit for the light cavalry are bought at the age of ten months and upwards by the Remount Department, which has thus taken, since the breeding of them was again permitted, 119, at an average price of 160 rupees. Fillies are kept by the Sillahdars, and by the time they are fit for work it is calculated each costs its owner 90 rupees.

14. *Feeding.*—The Sillahdar horses are generally in high condition, and daily receive each three or four seers of coolty, which is generally given at one meal, in the evening, when it is boiled, though some give one half only at that time, and the rest in the morning. The quantity is increased whenever a horse falls off in

condition, and some Sillahdars give their horses more grain in the hot season, when forage is scarce and expensive Regimentdars and Ressaldars have iron kettles, which hold 20 or 30 seers of grain, and one or two more of these are to be found in each Ressallah, but a great proportion of the coolty of a regiment is boiled in earthen vessels, and when these are not procurable, the whole is boiled in the iron kettles, which are lent for the purpose. Each Sillahdar boils the coolty for his own horse, unless he has relations in the regiment, in which case they club together, and boil the grain for all their horses at once, but none boil grain above once a day Coolty is preferred by them to any other pulse or grain, but if that is not procurable, they give chinna, baggera, paddy, or any other grain that their horses will eat

15 *Watering and Forage*—The horses are watered twice a day in the cold season, and three times a day when the weather is hot They are fed on green forage whenever procurable, as it is considered better for them than dry. Raggy straw is however found to be an excellent substitute for grass.

16. *Cost of Keep of a Horse.*—A Sillahdar pays on an average 2½ rupees a month for grain, and 2 rupees for forage, when purchased A nalbund is kept by each Ressallah, shoeing costs 14 annas for four feet, and one shoeing lasts a month if marching, and twice that time if at a station. Those men who employ a

Sillahdar may possibly bring up as a fresh horse one previously rejected by the military assistant, but not without running a great risk of detection, and it is certain that no imposition injurious to the interests of the service can exist, while the inspections are made as at present. It is obvious, therefore, that in marking the Sillahdars' horses no advantage could be obtained which would compensate for the annoyance and vexation it would give the men to see their horses branded

21. *Horse Appointments* —The horse appointments, which are uniform, and of the pattern established by Major Hunter, are in good preservation. A good khogheer, or native saddle, with bridle, stirrups, etc, complete, costs 12 rupees, and a zinposh, or saddle-cloth, 3 rupees 12 annas; the broad cloth of this is among the articles supplied by Government, of which a list will be found in statement A. The officers are desirous of establishing for each rank, corresponding to their new clothing, a superior description of zinposh, the pattern of which I purpose deciding upon at the approaching inspections. At present there is no difference between those of the officers and those of the Sillahdars, excepting in size. The weight of a good khogheer, complete with appointments as used on parade, is 40 lbs., a lighter one is apt to sore-back a horse. In light marching order, with line articles and three wood pegs, the weight is increased to 67 lbs, and in heavy marching order the weight is 81

lbs, as it includes a large bag of coarse cloth, containing a good-sized pot for boiling rice, a smaller one for making curry, a plate, a chemboo for water, one seer of rice, one-quarter seer of dhal, with ghee and curry stuff, also a large sheet used when bathing and for sleeping in. All these are carried on a forced march, and frequently on an ordinary one.

22. *Clothing and Equipments.*—The clothing and equipments of the Sillahdars are good and uniform. A fresh issue has lately been made of Madura turbands, scarlet broad cloth for augrackas, and grey cloth for trousers. The black leather slipper with spur attached, introduced in 1835, was found not to answer, being apt to fall off at exercise Applications being consequently made for permission to wear boots and buckle spurs, they have been issued, and are preferred to the slipper and fixed spur. A new uniform dress has been lately established for the officers, it is handsomer, and has much gratified them. The shape and colour of the dress of men and officers is the same. It consists of a red augracka or surtout, a red turband of Madura cloth, a plain white roomul (tied over the turband and under the chin), and a similar one worn as a sash, grey trousers, with boots and spurs The augracka of a Sillahdar is plain, that of an officer braided with gold. The turband of the Sillahdar is also plain, that of the officer striped with gold

23. *Arms.*—Every Sillahdar provides himself with a sword, and six men in each biradery have spears also. The spears are of a uniform pattern, supplied by Government, the iron part of which is paid for by the Sillahdars, and costs them 1½ rupees. The bamboo is issued gratis The swords are of various sorts, at the option of the men; but all are serviceable, as they pride themselves upon the sharpness and good condition of this weapon. On an average, a Sillahdar's sword does not cost more than 10 rupees, and many with excellent blades have been purchased for much less, owing to the number of men thrown out of service by the reductions in 1832 Those men to whom fire-arms are issued carry their ammunition in a pouch provided by themselves, and for which they pay about 1½ rupees each This pouch is attached to a leathern waist-belt, but without a shoulder-belt

24 *Fire-arms*—There are no fire-arms in use fit for service. 350 carbines, issued in 1837, are so old as to be almost unsafe, the slightest mistake in loading any one of them with ball would cause it to burst, and the locks are also worn out With little prospect of the Sillahdars being required for active service, it may not seem worth while to issue new fire-arms at present, but it may appear desirable that some should be kept in store, so as to be available in event of their being called out on actual service.

Unless procurable at a day's notice from the Madras Government, I would therefore suggest that a supply of approved fire-arms be procured from England and kept in reserve at Bangalore The old carbines will insure a certain number of men being practised in carrying this weapon, and serviceable fire-arms could thus be supplied when necessary As the Sillahdars themselves are anxious to have pistols, now in store, returned to them, I would also recommend that 150 pairs should be issued to each regiment; the use of them will accustom the horses to stand fire, and make the Sillahdars more formidable in their own estimation as well as in the eye of the people. From my own experience and observation, I consider that in event of any insurrection in this part of India, the Sillahdars, with good fire-arms, would be found the most efficient description of troops that could be employed, indeed, I am convinced that even with pistols, whatever the nature of the country, or however little adapted for the general movements of cavalry, they would soon put down any body of insurgents (unprotected by actual fortifications), if led by an active European officer, resolved to face all obstacles, and understanding well the native character in general, and more especially the peculiar habits and ideas of these troops

25. *Camp Equipage*—The Sillahdars provide their own camp equipage, whether in the field or on

the march from one station to another. A Regimentdar's tent costs on an average 200 rupees, a Ressaldar's 80 rupees, and a Jemadar's routee 15 rupees; the Sillahdars themselves either share a routee between four or five, or use a pall, generally made of a cambly or blanket, which is sufficient covering for one man, and is carried on a pony with the owner's other baggage Regimentdars are seldom without camels, and many of the Ressaldars also keep them, although, like the officers of inferior rank and the Sillahdars, their tents, etc, are not unfrequently carried by ponies or bullocks. Formerly the Rajah of Mysore allowed an elephant to each of the Regimentdars, with thirty rupees a month for the keep of the animal The men of the Pindara tribe almost always have their families with them, but those of other castes generally leave them behind, unless certain of remaining at a station for a year or more

26. *Parades, Field-Exercise, and Efficiency of the Sillahdars as Light Troops*—Regimental parades are restricted to once a week, which is found to be quite sufficient for the keeping up as much perfection in field-exercise as ought to be required from troops so constituted. The rapidity and correctness with which a Regimentdar puts his men through the usual changes of position in column and echelon is very creditable. A regiment is told off as our regular cavalry, and manœuvres in the same way, except that

the ressallahs, or troops, work independently of each other, that is, they have no squadrons composed of two troops. The horses are extremely well trained; there is no kicking or biting in the ranks. It is very rarely that a fall takes place, and the charges are almost always good. The men are partial to the use of the spear, and at a field-day, after being put through their few manœuvres, display in sham fights and skirmishes considerable proficiency in its management, as well as in the use of the fire-arms. Sillahdars seem best adapted for skirmishing and desultory fighting. Indeed, these men appear to possess an intuitive knowledge of this kind of warfare, being the direct descendants of the very Mysoreans who, in 1791, intercepted all intelligence and harassed our troops by so thoroughly clearing a populous country of its inhabitants and provisions, that neither man nor beast, nor even a bundle of dry forage, was to be found within reach of our army, and such was the vigilance of them in cutting off all communication, that no intelligence was received of the approach of the Mahratta army until it was actually in sight of that of Lord Cornwallis This efficiency was again shown in 1817. Sir John Malcolm states that when negotiating the peace with the Mahrattas, he discovered that the close pursuit kept up by the Mysore Sillahdars for upwards of twelve miles so distressed the enemy which our regular troops had routed at Maidpoor, as to have induced Holkar and his principal officers to solicit so early a settlement. It is also worthy of notice, as a proof of the fidelity of the Mysore Sillahdars, that of the 3000 of these men employed in the Mahratta country in 1803 and 1804, not one was missing, and of 4000 serving with our forces in the campaign of 1817, only two sowars are reported to have deserted, although upwards of three-fourths of them were more than three years absent from Mysore.

27. *Words of Command*—It has been requested by all the Regimentdars that the short English words of command should be employed instead of the long Persian sentences now in use The other officers and the men, being equally ignorant of both languages, wish too for the substitution of the shorter sentences Should it, therefore, meet with the Commissioner's approval, the English words of command for the manœuvres now executed could easily be furnished in the native characters. This change appears very desirable, as in case of emergency, if with a good cavalry officer at their head, they could then be worked in line with our regular troops.

28. *Prejudices to be Respected.*—All irregular horsemen have a strong prejudice against foot drill, branding their horses, and blunting their swords, and having ascertained that great discontent was caused in 1832 by attempting to introduce these and other

customs in use with our regular cavalry, I would hope that most positive orders might be given on the subject, lest at any future period the mistaken zeal of an officer commanding these troops should introduce changes which, being so repugnant to the Sillahdars, would soon destroy their attachment to Government It may also be observed that nothing is more galling to the feelings of the officers than the employment of confidential men to give information concerning occurrences in their respective regiments Such men must always be looked upon as spies, and treated as such by their officers and comrades, therefore the information obtained from them is by no means to be implicitly relied on, even where they themselves do not intentionally deceive The military assistant must himself at all times be on the watch to discover and correct irregularities, and his best method of doing so is by embracing every opportunity that presents itself of conversing privately both with officers and men, upon every subject connected with the service

29 *Reports and Returns.*—The following are the reports and returns sent in to the military assistant by the Regimentdars —Monthly Buramurd, or pay abstracts, Isumwar Hauzree, or muster-roll, Hauzree Goshwara, or general returns, Nugdy Jumma Khurch, or account-current of cash; Jinshee Jumma Khurch, or account-current of accoutrements, etc., Butwada

Putty, or acquittance-roll, and Weekly Covoyt Puttee, or present state on the day of exercise.

30. *Establishment and Pay of Seven Regiments* —The present strength of the Sillahdars is given in the accompanying statement, No 1, which also shows that the equalization of regiments (directed in the fifth paragraph of a letter from the Secretary to the Government of India, dated 31st March 1838) has been effected. A biradery now consists of 12 horses, a ressallah of 63 horses, and a regiment of 386 horses—such being the establishment sanctioned by the Commissioner in your letter, No 631, of 15th October 1842. The yearly pay of the present establishment of seven regiments is 761,216 rupees. Of this, 3240 rupees is extra pay, which having been drawn by some individuals under the Rajah's Government has been continued to them, deducting which, the monthly pay of each regiment of the present strength, viz., 386 horses, amounts to 9024 rupees, being on an average 23r. 6a for each man and horse As will be seen by statement No. 2 the actual cost to Government for the maintenance of the seven regiments, for the past official year, amounted to rupees 758,802 3·6, being 2447r. 7a. less than the actual pay of the same. This sum has reverted to Government, partly as fines, and partly as pay not drawn, pending the filling up of vacancies.

Sowar Cutcherry.—The present establishment of

the Sowar Cutcherry is given in statement No. 3, and it will be observed that, including the stationery and the keep of five elephants, the pay of this establishment for the past year was only 15,584 rupees 5 a At my recommendation, the Commissioner, in your letter, No 631, of 15th October 1842, directed that the two next vacancies occurring amongst the Goomashtahs, should not be filled up, thus reducing them from eight to six I find that I was premature in this suggestion, and that the present number of Goomashtahs is requisite for correctly keeping up the register of men and horses, furnishing returns and accounts, and answering the many references which the military assistant has almost daily to make respecting the claims of the numerous applicants for appointment to the horse. May I therefore request that the order for their reduction may be rescinded? An English writer, whose pay was formerly drawn in the Hoozoor cutcherry, has been transferred to the Sowar cutcherry; and I take this opportunity of requesting that an adequate establishment of English writers may be assigned to the cutcherry, in which I am at present compelled to employ extra assistance, to prevent the business from falling in arrears. There were 294 letters despatched from the office in 1843, but this correspondence is a very small portion of the English writer's work, which, comprising as it does the registering in English of every man and horse in the service, making out the monthly returns of each regiment of Sillahdars and Barr, also quarterly returns of the accoutrements and ammunition of the Barr, translating the monthly abstracts of the Sillahdars and Barr, and of all inquiries and trials referred to the decision of the Commissioner, etc, is more than any one man can do. The want of medical aid when the military assistant is on inspection tours has been felt by the servants of the cutcherry, and as most of the stations of regiments are at a considerable distance from the head-quarters of any of the superintendents, there is no possibility of good advice being speedily procured It seems, therefore, desirable that an apothecary should be attached to the Sowar establishment, as, when violent disease breaks out in a regiment (which frequently occurs with fever and cholera), he might, when not elsewhere wanted, be sent at once to give advice and assistance in arresting its progress, and so afford the Sillahdars another proof of the care taken of them by Government And still further to improve the respectability of the military cutcherry, I would add that a cutcherry tent is very desirable, no accommodation being sanctioned for the military cutcherry when on circuit, although tents are allowed to the cutcherry of the superintendent of a division

32. *Pensioners*—There are three classes of pensioners (*vide* statement No. 4) for whom pay is drawn through the Sowar cutcherry Many of these

are influential men, whose good-will it must of course be the object of Government to retain. Of these pensioners, the Bayross Mootfurkhat, including the Kurabutdars, may be classed as the first; they are, with two exceptions, all Mussulmans, and many of them related to Tippoo, as the word Kurabutdar expresses, but several claim no such relationship, being only descendants of those who held the highest offices in his court. The Ross Mootfurkhats is composed of men of equally good families, and includes persons of other castes, though principally Mussulmans; they were compelled by the Rajah to keep horses, but this obligation being only to add to his mounted retinue, has been cancelled, as they never did any duty, were badly mounted, and no register was kept of their horses. The Nonpurvureshees, the third class of these pensioners, is a charitable establishment for disabled Sillahdars, or families of Sillahdars killed on service. The total amount paid to these pensioners at the date of Major Hunter's report was 4345 rupees; the present amount is 3208 rupees 4a., as seen in statement No. 4, a reduction of 1136 rupees 12a. having been occasioned by deaths, and by (at their own requests) the transfer of thirty-six pensioners to the effective establishment of Sillahdars.

33. *Cost of the whole Sowar establishment.*—By statement No. 5 it will be seen that the pay of the

Sowar establishment (including stationery and all the pensioners), for the past official year, cost the Government rupees 814,768 : 15 1, and that batta and contingent charges amounted to rupees 1142 11 : 9. These seven regiments furnish 2702 horses, and that portion of the cutcherry who keep horses, and may be compared with the staff of our regular army, increases the Sillahdar force to 2720 effective men and horses; which force is kept efficient, and about two-thirds of it ready to move on the shortest notice, at the cost above shown to Government, *i.e.* at the rate of rupees 23 : 11 . 3¼ per month for each man and horse, when only the effective establishment is calculated. If Nonpurvursh pensioners are included, the rate is increased to rupees 23 · 12 7 per month, and when all pensioners are included, an efficient man and horse will appear to cost Government rupees 25 0 8½ per month The entire Sillahdar force could not be available for field service under two, or even three months, as that time would be necessary to replace mares in foal, and assemble those men absent on furlough.

34. *Policy of maintaining the Sillahdar Horse*—According to the terms of the treaty of 1807, the Mysore horse were to be kept up to the number of 4000,[1] whereas at present they are 1280 under that strength, the great change in the condition of India since that period, would, however, appear to render

[1] 3500 Sillahdars, 500 Barrgheers

any increase to the present force an unnecessary expense; were it not so much the object of Government to retain the attachment of its subjects, by continuing to provide for the families of the higher classes, numbers of whom, formerly supported on the pensions granted to individuals amongst them, are, by the death of the recipients, and the consequent reversion of the pension to Government, in a state of poverty, and even in many instances destitution. This Sillahdar force, to quote the words of the Government of India, "has been substituted for a far more numerous and expensive armament, to which the chiefs of the country were accustomed to look as amongst the means of securing a provision for their families, and the too narrow curtailment of this resource seems likely to produce a disaffection and discontent, for which any consequent saving in money would be a very inadequate compensation."[1] There cannot be a doubt of the truth of this remark, and the Mysore horse is considered by all those eligible for it as by far the best service in the country, affording the most

[1] I may here mention that the whole of my policy in India, more or less, was moulded on conformity to this principle, and the carrying of it out, and I do not believe that in any other service in India, under European control, native family claims have of late years been so much recognised as in that of Mysore, and, well aware of my attention to this point, the old military families of Mysore have, with reason, considered me to be their best friend I say "with reason," for during the seventeen years that I had the enlistments and promotions of the large Mysore force left so much to my own discretion, I ever did the utmost in my power, with due regard to the interests of the Government, to perpetuate in such families the rank and position held by their ancestors

secure prospect of a provision for them and their families; and since pensions are no longer continued to the heirs of those dying among the Mootfurkhats, the whole of this influential class of men look to employment as Sillahdars as the only hope of support for their children and dependants. Every endeavour has of late been made by native officers in our regular service to procure employment for their sons as Sillahdars, but so strictly has the rule against their admission been adhered to, that on a recent occasion when a pensioned native officer of my own regiment sought for instances of its infringement, in the hope of inducing me to accede to the entertainment of his son as a Sillahdar, he found that there were but three such cases, and I showed him that none of the three could have been received into our own regular cavalry The frequent introduction of such men, to the prejudice, as it would be, of the best families, in Mysore, could not fail to produce some discontent in the country, and might even cause general disaffection in the service. Major Hunter considered that the present Mootfurkhats and some of their sons would form, if embodied into a couple of Ressallahs, a select and valuable addition to the Sillahdars, an opinion which I also held, until convinced of its incorrectness, from finding that the few men of this class recently entertained possess none of the energy or expert horsemanship shown by the sons of old Sillahdars, who are trained from their childhood for the service. Although I consider that if embodied into a separate troop their habits of idleness would render them an inefficient corps, yet, as the example of those with whom they are associated must have a considerable influence upon their habits and character, I have little doubt that recruits taken from this class of men will in a short time become equal to the rest of the Sillahdars. With a view, therefore, to relieve the families of some of these pensioners, and to afford a provision for a few young men who have strong claims on the Mysore Government, by acting in the spirit of the above quoted remark from the Government of India, I would beg leave to suggest to the Commissioner an increase this year of a certain number of men to each regiment, and would propose that this increase should be effected by appointing at least two additional Sillahdars to each Ressallah[1] This would give employment to 84 men, many of whom, though of high rank, are in the greatest distress, at an expense to Government of 1764 rupees per month, a portion of which would of course be met by a reduction in the pension list, arising both from deaths, and from a few additional transfers to this effective establishment.

35 *Present and former condition of Sillahdars.*— It is impossible to ascertain what was the exact pay drawn by a Sillahdar under the administration of his

1 This suggestion was adopted by the Commissioner, and was carried into effect by his orders.

Highness the Rajah, as the rates were arbitrary, and the issues of pay uncertain, the amount paid to officers seems to have been still more irregular, and to have depended entirely upon his Highness's private sentiments toward each individual The monthly pay (*vide* statement No 5) of a Sillahdar, as established by Poorniah, was considered to be rupees 189 14 a year, or 15 3 2 a month each man, but the only way in which a comparison can be justly drawn between the former and present cost of these troops, is by ascertaining the expense to Government at both periods, of keeping up a certain number, and to this end, in statement No 7 is given the actual disbursement to the Sowar cutcherry for maintaining horses and men, including Sillahdars, officers, and Mootfurkhats, from 1820 to 1831. The average monthly cost to Government is thus shown to have varied from rupees 22 7 11 to 19 13.2 for each mounted man The Rajah's Barrgheer horse, of which 500 were kept up, are not included in this list, they not having been attached to the Sowar cutcherry On referring to this statement, and comparing it with what is shown in paragraph 33 of this Report, the present appears to be the more expensive establishment; but it must be remembered that the useless Mootfurkhat formerly swelled the number of horses, and that they are still paid out of the Sowar cutcherry, though no longer mounted. The Sillahdars too, who were formerly the oppressors of the ryots, and whose entrance into a village was dreaded as that of a body of marauders, their uncertain support being in a great measure derived from pillage, are now, being paid with regularity, enabled honestly to procure supplies for themselves and their horses, and being no longer permitted to injure or oppress the inhabitants, are looked upon by all as welcome protectors, and purchasers for the produce of their ground. Although the condition of the Sillahdars and inferior officers is so much improved, such is not the case with the Regimentdars and Moonib. I am of opinion that their pay is not sufficient to enable them to live in a manner becoming their situations, without having recourse to other means, and it is much less than they formerly received, partly as pay, partly as authorized perquisites, but chiefly gained by cheating the men, I would therefore strongly recommend that the pay of these officers be increased from 250 rupees to 400 rupees, which would amount to within 100 rupees of the sum lately drawn by the two Buckshees, and would but place them on an equality with officers of corresponding rank in his Highness the Nizam's service, in which a Ressaldar (the highest native rank) receives 500 Hydrabad rupees a month The amount of batta, when these troops are employed out of the Mysore country, is half the pay of each rank. A statement of the number of men of each caste accompanies this Report.

36. *1st Regiment.*—The 1st Regiment is commanded by Regimentdar Goolam Hoossain Khan. This regiment furnished most of the detachments of the Mysore division from July 1840 to December 1843, when it was assembled at Hassen It has been temporarily ordered to the Nuggur division in consequence of the disturbances in the southern Mahratta country, but when the present excitement is at an end will return to Hassen. The Regimentdar is a man of high character and connexions, well disposed, and kind to those under his command; and though by no means a smart or intelligent officer, he is on the whole fairly qualified for his situations, being well spoken of by his men, who are happy and contented, and the regiment is in good order. This Regimentdar entered the regiment as Sillahdar in 1806 on the pay of twelve pagodas; he was appointed Ressaldar in 1823, and Regimentdar in 1835. Ressaldar Soobba Row Ghorepuday is the smartest officer in this regiment, his father was a Regimentdar. The other Ressaldars are, however, perfectly fit for their situations, with the exception of Rayajee Ghorepuday, who, besides being of a questionable character, is from bad health very seldom fit for duty.

37. *2d Regiment*—The 2d Regiment is commanded by Regimentdar Krishna Row, he is the senior Regimentdar in the service, and the eldest son of the late Buckshee Annajee Row, he was raised to his present

rank in 1816, having entered the service as Sillahdar on a salary of 25 pagodas in 1812. I am afraid that he deserves no better character than that given of him by the late Colonel Conway, with whom I agree in considering this man as an "intriguing character, and capable of deceit and imposition." He is rich, and has the character of being covetous; he has, however, many friends in the service, and although the only Regimentdar who has not a good character, he is disliked by but a small portion of his men, and on the whole keeps his regiment in good order The Ressaldars of the regiment are all fit for their situations, though not one of them deserves mention as being superior to the rest. The regiment has supplied the detachments of the Bungalore division since February 1842; it was before that stationed at Closepett, and is now under orders for the Nuggur division.

38. *3d Regiment.*—The 3d Regiment is commanded by Regimentdar Trimul Row; he is in every respect the most intelligent and smartest Regimentdar in the service, and the best qualified for the discharge of any important duty. He was appointed Sillahdar in 1825 on forty-five rupees a month, and in 1840, on the death of his brother Regimentdar, Sreenevas Row, succeeded him in the command of his regiment. Trimul Row is not more than forty years of age; he is rather more strict with his men than any of the

other Regimentdars, but is both liked and respected by them, and has the character of being a very just man. This regiment has been employed in the Chittledroog division since 1840, chiefly on detachment duty, and is now under orders to assemble at the town of Chittledroog. Ressaldar Chintamony Row, son of the late Buckshee Annuppa, promises to be the best Ressaldar in the regiment, the others are all, however, sufficiently qualified. Ressaldar Ramasing is not so much liked by his men as the others, being a man of violent temper

39. *4th Regiment*—The 4th Regiment is commanded by Regimentdar Chenderrow Runnowry. He entered the service as Jemadar in 1800 on twenty pagodas, was promoted Ressaldar in 1823, and appointed Regimentdar in room of his father, Rughoonath Row Runnowry, in 1824 He served in the Deckan with General Wellesley and Sir J Hyslop, and in 1830 was employed in Nuggur He is considered the most experienced soldier in the service, and being rich, and spending his money freely, he is greatly liked by his officers and men, and keeps his regiment in high order. He has also good Ressaldars There is not a better Ressaldar in the service than Nuggur Ram Row, and the Regimentdar's brother, Sutwajee Runnowry, is also a good officer This regiment has been employed in the Nuggur division since June 1840, but is now under orders for Closepett, and will march

thither after the disturbances in the Mahratta country are quelled.

40. *5th Regiment.*—The 5th Regiment is commanded by Regimentdar Hussenali Khan, and what I have said of the other Mussulman Regimentdar, Goolam Hoossain Khan, is equally applicable to him, although as an efficient commanding officer I would decidedly give this man the preference. He entered the service in 1812 as Jemadar, was made Ressaldar in 1816, and Regimentdar in 1841. His regiment is in high order, and with the exception of Ressaldar Jamioollabdeen Khan, who is an indifferent officer and a man of very questionable character, the Ressaldars are good men, and well qualified for their office. This regiment has been assembled at Mudgherry since December 1843, it was in the neighbourhood of Toomkoor from November 1841, and has now marched to the frontier in consequence of the state of affairs in the southern Mahratta country It is under orders to furnish the detachments of the Bangalore division on the expiration of its present employment

41. *6th Regiment*—The 6th Regiment is commanded by Regimentdar Babarowmanay. He entered the service as Ressaldar in 1810, and was promoted to Regimentdar in 1837; he is a smart, active officer, and very anxious to merit the approbation of Government. When addressing his officers he is unfortunately apt to forget himself, and use language hurtful to their

feelings, as they have more than once represented to me; but he always expresses his regret for having given offence, and in every other respect bears the highest character, especially for integrity in money matters. This regiment has been at Closepett since June 1841, and is in very good order; it is now under orders to furnish the detachments of the Chittledroog division, but in consequence of the disturbed state of the southern Mahratta country, it marched for the frontier on the 18th October 1844 Ressaldar Shevajeemanay is at present under suspension, by order of the Commissioner The other five Ressaldars are all competent for the discharge of their respective duties

42. *7th Regiment.*—The 7th Regiment is commanded by Regimentdar Bangalore Krishna Row, a smart intelligent man and zealous officer He entered the service in 1809, was appointed a Ressaldar in 1813, and Regimentdar in 1842, has always borne a good character, and is very much liked and respected by his officers and men. Ressaldar Booden Khan Kulleany is the only Ressaldar in this regiment who has not a fair character; the other five are very respectable men, and the high state of the regiment is sufficient proof that all do their duty. This regiment had been stationed at Krishna Rajakutta, or at Nunjenagood, from May 1840 to November 1843, when it was broken up to furnish the detachments of the

Mysore division, and the head-quarters were removed to Yedatory; but as the 1st Regiment has been removed from Hassen, it is now under orders to assemble there.

43. *Sowar Cutcherry*.—The servants of the Sowar Cutcherry are in general equal to their duties The head Goomashtah, Nagesha Row, is a good man of business, but has the character of being dishonest, and it would not be wise to place much confidence in him. Of the Moonib Hunuamunta Row I have a high opinion As a Regimentdar he is equal to Trimul Row, and as head of the cutcherry he is a most valuable public servant

44 I trust that the preceeding remarks will be found to explain the system pursued by me, and to show that in dispensing with the intervention of Buckshees nothing has been done calculated to lessen the confidence and respect which it is so essential that the Sillahdars, as well as other troops, should entertain towards their own officers. The Sillahdars are decidedly well affected towards us. Much reliance may be placed on their courage and obedience, and there can be no doubt but they would willingly march to any province, however distant, where their services might be required in the field. As a disciplined body they are not, of course, to be in any way compared to our light cavalry, but as scouts or foragers, for the attack of insurgents or marauders, or for the pursuit

of disciplined forces (when once defeated by our regular troops), they will be found most efficient—though, like all natives, much can never be expected from them unless they are acting under the eye of a good European officer.

I have the honour to be, Sir, your most obedient servant,

A MACLEOD,
Military Assistant to the Commissioner

MILITARY ASSISTANT'S OFFICE, BANGALORE,
27*th October* 1844

As my fears of India, my promise to my old regiment, my experience of irregular troops, and my intimate knowledge of native character have induced me to give my ideas to the public in the hope of doing some good, I trust a few pages bearing on the *conduct* of the Sillahdars during the mutiny will not be uninteresting to the reader, seeing that I have so minutely described them as a military system of India yeomanry very much similar to our own English yeoman, except in pay.

The first demand made for the services of the Mysore cavalry, out of their own country, after the breaking out of the mutiny of the Bengal army, came from Madras on the 21st July 1857, when 500 were applied for to serve with a moveable column in the ceded districts. I speedily collected and equipped for service two regiments, each of 264 picked men and horses; but on the 5th August, when they were approaching the frontier, the very day I myself was proceeding by express to join them there, I was ordered to recall them in consequence of a requisition that came by telegraph to Sir Mark Cubbon from the Secretary to the Government of India, in these words —"Send 2000 Mysore horse as soon as possible, under command of Lieutenant-Colonel Macleod, to the Bengal Presidency, *via* Bellary, Nagpore, and Mirzapore. Raise other horse to replace these 2000 More by post." This news quickly spread, creating intense excitement and delight throughout the force, and also throughout the country, each of the multitude of candidates for enlistment hoping that the increase of demand might provide for himself; and this excitement was not confined to the Sillahdars, and the class of men of which they are chiefly composed, but was shared by the infantry, as will be seen by the two following letters —

"No 228—To the Secretary to the Commissioner, etc

"Bangalore, *7th August* 1857

"Sir,—I have the honour to report, for the information of the Commissioner, that the intelligence that two thousand Sillahdars were to proceed to Bengal has been received with the utmost enthusiasm by all ranks, nor is the desire to serve against the mutineers confined to the horse I was this day waited upon by Syed Booden, the Buckshee of the Mysore infantry, who came the representative of that branch, and assured me that the feeling of loyalty to the British Government was universal amongst his men, and that in particular the 1st and 2d battalions were most anxious to accompany the Sillahdars to Upper India. I informed him that the requisition was confined to cavalry, but that it would give me great pleasure to make the wishes of his men known to the Commissioner It is needless to assure the Commissioner that, although from the beginning of the rebellion in the north-west I have been fully aware of the existence of these sentiments throughout the Mysore troops, yet I have carefully avoided in any way leading them to volunteer their services, nor had I the slightest idea, until the Buckshee presented himself on behalf of the men under his command, that it was the intention to do so — I have the honour, etc A MACLEOD, M A"

The following is the reply to my letter —

"No 538 —TO THE MILITARY ASSISTANT TO THE COMMISSIONER

"BANGALORE, *8th Aug* 1857

"SIR,—In reply to your letter, No 228, of the 7th instant, stating that Syed Booden, the Barr Buckshee, made a representation to you that the 1st and 2d battalions of Barr were anxious to accompany the Sillahdar force on field service to Bengal, I have the honour, by the desire of the Commissioner, to request that you will inform that officer that this spontaneous representation is most gratifying, and will be duly brought to the notice of Government, but that their services will not be found necessary, as British troops are immediately expected in such numbers as will be more than sufficient to put down all opposition, and restore order throughout the disturbed provinces —I have the honour, etc.

"F. CUNNINGHAM, *Secretary*."

The general opinion held by Europeans on this march may be summed up in the words of an eminent Bengal civilian, the Honourable H. B Devereux, possessing great knowledge of the natives, and of varied Indian experience —"Macleod's march through the country with such a body of horse will be like pouring oil on troubled waters" But the most remarkable volunteer was Abdoolah Bin Hassan, a man well known in India as possessing remarkable energy and intelligence, strongly attached to the English, and of high standing in his own country, and a man to whom General Stalker, when going in command of the Persian expedition of 1855, had offered a confidential appointment in the Intelligence Department With Abdoolah Ben Hassan I had been well acquainted, as I had purchased from his fine lot of Arabs for many years On hearing of the order for my march to Bengal, he came (on the 6th) to my house, expressing his strong desire to accompany me; showing that he could at once undertake to muster 200 first-rate horses, for which he and the other Arab and Persian dealers had refused the highest price given by Government (700 rupees each); and representing that he had on the spot a few reliable men, and that in passing through Hydrabad he would have the pick of the Arabs in the Nizam's country, as all would flock to him, because their chief there was of the same family as himself, although of a lower branch of it. He said to me that he and his countrymen were bound by their religion to fight for the English, because England had fought for their Sultan, the head of their Mohammedan religion, and had prevented Russia from taking Turkey, etc. Should his services have been accepted, he expected for himself the rank and pay of a Regimentdar, and that his followers should be paid and officered in the same way as the Sillahdars To my painful regret, Sir Mark Cubbon would not entertain Abdoolah's proposal. Shortly after he went to Arabia to purchase horses for our remount, being thus employed by the Government of Madras, which proved its good opinion of him by advancing him a lac of rupees (£10,000) for that purpose, without other security than that of his well-known character.

I need not say that there was much to do in suddenly preparing and collecting, in the middle of the south-west monsoon, so large a cavalry force for field service and a march of about 1200 miles. But difficulties were easily and speedily overcome Officers and men were all alike zealous on the occasion, and each strove to outvie the other in the work of preparation

By a few new enlistments, and by making selections from the seven regiments (at that time each mustering 392 of all ranks), I had ready seven excellent regiments of irregular cavalry, consisting each of 296 men. There were in all 2072 right well mounted and clothed, and very tolerably armed, hardy horsemen. These men had an hereditary love for such service, having had among them traditions and recollections of their warfare with, and pursuit of, the Peishwa in 1817-18, and the thought that they were now to be engaged in a warfare against that Peishwa's very adopted son, the now notorious and infamous Nana Sahib, inspired all ranks with double enthusiasm On the other hand, the fidelity of these men to the British Government was equally enthusiastic, as they had for years received pay from it, and had their interests and customs generally protected without much interference; and that their loyalty would be unwavering and steadfast was thoroughly guaranteed, from their knowing that their lands and possessions, though left behind them, would remain secure and untouched, whilst during their absence their wives and children would be supported by the regular payment of their *batta*, and, in the event of their death, would be provided for by the usual allowances.

All the arrangements for the long march were almost completed, when on the 16th of August all was stopped by the receipt of a telegram to the Commissioner, from the Military Secretary to the Government at Madras

It was to all, men and officers alike, a bitter disappointment, to be thus sent back again—in order to be "scattered over the country as a military police," to use the Commissioner's own words. They had gone to heavy expenses, yet not one asked to be repaid money that had been so unfortunately spent. It was not of course desirable to repay them for expenses incurred in mere preparations for active service, yet I felt it but just to bring to notice the exertions they had made on the occasion. And when applying for the sanction of the Commissioner for the enlistment of a few additional Sillahdars and Burgheers, I wrote. "The desire for service on this occasion has been so general and enthusiastic, that in many instances the horses have been purchased at exorbitant prices, and by the sale and mortgage of family jewels and property; and it is a question whether any troops ever felt more disappointment at a countermand, after being ordered on service, than has been experienced by the Sillahdars on this occasion."[1]

From the officers in charge of the four divisions of Mysore, I received hearty co-operation in every way possible.

The Sillahdars were all returned to their usual detached posts, and every idea of their employment out of the Mysore country apparently given up, when, a third time, came a sudden and unexpected requisition for some of them. On the morning of the 10th of November, the Commissioner gave me to read the

[1] The Commissioner on this occasion kindly sanctioned all new enlistments, as an increase to the established number of Sillahdars

following telegram of that date, just received by him from the Military Secretary to the Government of Madras —"It is proposed to move General Whitlock's column to Nagpore. Can you give Mysore horse (say one thousand) to replace this column in the ceded districts? If you wish three or four officers to serve with them, they can be given from the 8th Cavalry."

I at once told Sir Mark Cubbon that I could undertake to have 300 Sillahdars at Bellary within twenty days, a second 300 in ten days more, and 400 in other ten days.

It is not necessary that I should give a detailed account of the services these men rendered, or of the causes that led me to avail myself of sick-certificate to return to my native country for a short time. The latter is far too much of a *private* nature to admit of publication, or to effect any good without doing a greater harm. After fifteen months' absence in England I returned to India, and I venture to hope that the following testimonials prove the efficiency and bravery of the 1000 Sillahdars which, before availing myself of sick-certificate, and agreeable to the orders of my superiors, I placed under Captain Newberry and Lieutenant Stewart, both of the unfortunate 8th Light Cavalry.

From MAJOR J E HUGHES, *commanding Kurnoob Moveable Column, Camp at Thorapore, 26th February* 1858, *to the* ADJUTANT-GENERAL *of the Army, Fort Saint George*

"SIR,—I have the honour to acknowledge the receipt of your letter,[1] No 83, of the 17th instant, and in reply thereto beg leave to report, for the information of His Excellency the Commander-in-Chief, that the charge in which Captain Newberry was killed and Lieutenant Stewart wounded did not come under my own observation, in consequence of the charge being made in a hollow, and about 200 yards' distance from where I was engaged with the artillery and skirmishers

"On the death of Captain Newberry being reported to me, which it was immediately done, I at once asked where were the Sillahdars, and was informed that the speed the two officers charged at was so great that the Sillahdars could not keep up with them, such was the general opinion of those that witnessed the charge, and as the enemy had no time to plunder or mutilate the body of Captain Newberry, I considered that the Sillahdars must have been well up to have prevented it The two officers rode nearly together Lieutenant Stewart received his wound first, and when defending himself Captain Newberry rode over a bank into a tope, with a fall on the inside of about five feet He entered on the south side, on doing this he received a volley from the enemy, which must have immediately brought him down, for there his body lay; his horse received three ball wounds

"A badar, one of the enemy, was in the act of taking off his sword and belt, when Sillahdar Bauboo Ram Sillenka

[1] Requiring an explicit statement as to how the Mysore horse behaved in the charge in which Captain Newberry was killed and Lieutenant Stewart wounded.

prevented it, and killed him on the spot; other Sillahdars, with Bauboorow Manay, Regimentdar, and Venkutraum Manay, Jemadar, quickly followed in

"Just at this time, Lieutenant Doveton, with his troop of the 3d Light Cavalry, charged through the tope, and on passing by the body of Captain Newberry, who he saw was dead, he observed several Sillahdars standing around him.

"I have carefully examined the ground, and am of opinion that on Captain Newberry's riding over the bank, a volley, which I remarked, was discharged at him, and that the enemy had no time to reload their muskets and matchlocks before the Mysore horse entered.

"The medical officer's statement, which I beg leave to enclose, will show that the volley was a severe one Lieutenant Stewart, in cutting down a rohilla and fighting with another, was severely wounded outside the tope, but fortunately kept his seat, and was saved by the approach of his men. I have called upon Lieutenant Stewart for a report, which I beg leave to attach

"It is my opinion, and also the general opinion, that the Mysore horse behaved fully as well as an undisciplined body of men could have done, the ground they charged over was down hills, very rough, and did not admit of their charging abreast.

"I therefore trust that His Excellency the Commander-in-Chief will consider this explanation satisfactory, especially as I must say that the Sillahdars have, during the time they have been under my command, evinced the greatest willingness to perform their duties"

Extract of Letter to the DEPUTY ASSISTANT ADJUTANT-GENERAL, *Ceded Districts, Bellary*

"SIR,—The field force lately employed under my command against rebel Beam Row and his followers having this day returned to Bellary, I do myself the honour of reporting to you, for the information of the Major-General commanding the ceded districts, the very useful service which was performed by the Mysore horse attached to the force, especially by the Ressalah that were actually employed with it on the 1st and 2d of June at the storming and taking of Copal.

"2 From daybreak of the morning of the 31st, till the evening of the following day, five Ressalahs, as per margin,[1] were employed in investing the fort and hills, together with a squadron of the 5th Light Cavalry, covering a space of seven or eight miles

"3 They had little or no food during the whole time, and no cover whatever, and not only in this instance, but in every other, they evinced the utmost willingness to perform any duties required of them.

"4 Their great watchfulness on this occasion considerably tended to prevent the escape of any rebels

"5 When directed to proceed on any duty, I have invariably found them ready to start in a few minutes

"6 Tookojee Row Manay, son of Regimentdar Bauboo Row Manay, late Ressaldar of the 6th Regiment, who was in March last discharged for inattention to orders, attached himself to me during the whole of the 31st of May and 1st of June, when employed in the field, and made himself generally useful in conveying orders, etc, to the Mysore horse

"7 He deeply regrets his previous misconduct, therefore should his repentance, and the excellent behaviour of his father's regiment when under my command, meet the approval of the Major-General, I respectfully beg leave to request that the late conduct of Toorkojee Row Manay may also come under his favourable consideration, with a

[1] 2d Regiment, Kristna Row, 4 Ressalahs
6th do Bauboo Row, 1 do
7th do Lutchmon Row, 1 do, employed on the second day only

view to his being reinstated in his former position as Ressaldar, should doing such not be injurious to the service

J. HUGHES,
Major Commanding Field Force

"BELLARY, 14*th June* 1858"

Extract, paragraph 12, *of a Letter from* LIEUTENANT-COLONEL MALCOLM, *Commanding Field Force, to the address of the* ASSISTANT ADJUTANT-GENERAL, *Southern Division of the Army, Belgaum, dated 7th June* 1858

"12 A party of twelve Mysore horse, who had accidentally joined me, also behaved most gallantly, and their Jemadar, Tookajei Byajei Cuddum, was severely wounded I saw him and one or two of his men (his son among the number) among the leading men, charging a band of nine of the rebels, who would not give up their arms, but fought desperately behind some mounds (True extract)

"MALCOLM,
"*Lieut-Colonel Commanding Field Force*

From OFFICER COMMANDING CEDED DISTRICTS *to* SIR MARK CUBBON

"BELLARY, 24*th June* 1858

"MY DEAR GENERAL,—I have the pleasure to send you copy of a letter from Lieutenant-Colonel Malcolm, bearing further testimony to the excellent conduct of the Mysore horse, also a telegram from the gallant Jemadar Byajei Cuddum, asking permission to have his leg amputated Of course, to save the poor fellow's life, I recommended him to submit to the operation

"D MACLEOD, *M-Genl*

"*To* General Sir Mark Cubbon,
Commissioner, etc"

The above brave Jemadar died during the operation. He was a Maharatta Brahmin. He was proceeding on escort duty with his Biradery of twelve men, and, hearing firing in the neighbourhood, he went and found the Bombay column engaged with rebels. At once this experienced old soldier placed himself and Biradery under the orders of the English commander. I was informed by his son, who was promoted as a matter of course to the Jemadaree, while a younger brother succeeded to his Sillahdaree, that his father died a happy death, in the firm belief that his loss would not be felt by his family, for the Circar (Government) was sure to provide for all he left dear to him in this world In telling this story of a brave Sowar, I am reminded of a less glorious death which I witnessed, showing how calmly and happily native Indians die when their families are provided for. This death was that of a Duffadar of Peons, also a Maharatta. In the year 1838, when I was in full charge of the Nuggur division of Mysore, out shooting near Simoga, my head-quarters, I wounded a large panther, which on the way to its cave fell in with and knocked over the unfortunate Duffadar of Peons. The man was naked above the waist, and the only injury seemingly done to him was a few scratches on his right shoulder; but he declared that he felt the poison of the brute's nails enter his blood, and that he would not live to see another day. Drawing his dagger, he attempted to follow the panther into the cave. From doing this, however, he was prevented, and I shot the animal through its heart, at which the unfortunate Duffadar showed savage but calm delight. Hoping to comfort him, I offered to ride into Simoga for the doctor To this he and his family and relations so much objected that I saw the best I could do was to please them So on the spot I put his Duffadar's belt over the shoulder of his eldest son, who was a Peon, and with the belt of this newly promoted Duffadar I adorned the second son, an arrangement highly applauded by the Duffadar and all present Yet the poor man declared that he felt the panther's poison, and was sure to die before next day. Promising to give him *next day* the Government reward of 15 Rs for a panther killed, I rode away home On riding to the village nèxt morning, I was told by the family that their father had died, as he said he would, before sunrise, and I may remark that nothing, indeed, can make an Indian so loyal to our Government as his knowledge of the fact that his family thus are provided for after his death, and any arrangements, from any motives whatever, which snap this tie between our Government and the natives of India, are sure to be ruinous, and finally will lead to disastrous consequences.

The following are General Lovell's Reports on the Sillahdars.—

"*To* MAJOR-GENERAL ALLAN, C B, *Commanding Mysore Division of the Army*

"SIR,—In obedience to the Commander-in-Chief's instructions, conveyed in the Adjutant General's letter, No 2172, under date 21st April 1841, I have the honour to report, that I repaired to Closepett and reviewed and inspected the two regiments of Sillahdar horse assembled there

"1. The number in the field amounted to 726 of all ranks, they appeared with great uniformity, both as to dress and appointments, excepting their being armed with various weapons, being lances, swords, long muskets, and old-fashioned carbines

"2 They executed movements with greater precision than I could have imagined

"3 *Horses* — Both regiments were extremely well mounted, chiefly on mares, some as fine mares as could be wished to be seen, their cattle altogether were fully equal to the Light Cavalry, and the whole extremely well managed

"4 *Arms*—Their arms were various They appeared to wish to have more carbines, those they at present have are of a bad sort, and much out of order There are a number of carbines, formerly belonging to the Light Dragoons, in store at the fort in Bangalore, of the short pattern, that might be made available

"5. *Appointments*—Those armed with fire-arms are badly off for pouches, which might also be made good from the store above mentioned

"6 The saddlery appeared to be good and serviceable, and of the same pattern, as also the horse-cloths

"7. The clothing was uniform, and the pattern good, but much worn If the men could receive new clothing gratis, once in four years, it would be a great boon, their pay not admitting the often purchasing of new coats

"8 The Sillahdars were all regularly paid, at the rate of 20 rupees a month, finding everything themselves The men appeared satisfied, and I am informed that a very good *esprit* pervades them, and their services may be depended on There is one boon they seem to wish, that is, to be allowed to breed from the mares, substituting, if necessary, another mare of equal goodness in the room during the time of breeding, and having seen the produce of some mares whilst formerly permitted to breed, I think it would be the means of insuring a good breed of horses in the country The men seem extremely fond of their horses

"9 The whole arrangement does great credit to Captain Macleod and the native officers he employed under him — I have the honour to be, etc etc

"L LOVELL,
Brigadier Inspecting Officer

"CLOSEPETT, 25*th June* 1841"

"SERINGAPATAM, 7*th July* 1841

"*To the* MAJOR-GENERAL *Commanding Mysore Division*

"SIR,—In obedience to your orders, and the letters of instruction, Nos 264 and 289, I this day concluded the inspection of the two Sillahdar regiments of horse assembled here for that purpose

"I have the honour to make the following remarks —

"*General appearance* —The two regiments mustered 629 in the field, 74 being absent on command in the north

"Their general appearance was equally good with those I last had the honour to inspect at Closepett, the men were perhaps larger in size

"*Horses* —They were equally well mounted, on generally splendid mares, which were well managed and broken

"Their clothes were uniform, and of the same pattern as those I last inspected

"*Arms and Appointments*—They were armed like the other corps, with lances, swords, and long carbines It seemed the wish that those armed with lances should each have a pistol, an arrangement which I much approve of The others required some new carbines, most of those now in use being unserviceable, although the men had endeavoured to get them repaired at their own expense, also a number of pouches are required Indeed, the remarks I made in my former report are equally applicable to these The men appeared in good spirit, and are well satisfied, requesting only the same boon as I had the honour to request in my last report The commanding officers of all the corps seemed to quite understand their business I have the honour to be, etc etc L LOVELL, *Inspecting Officer*"

"(True copy)
"J ALLAN, *Major-General*
Commanding Mysore Dn of the Army"

"COONGHULL, 12*th July* 1841

"*To* COLONEL M CUBBON, *Commissioner in Mysore*

"SIR,—I have the honour to inform you that I this day inspected a regiment of Sillahdars assembled at this place, under the command of Regimentdar Tirmul Row, it mustered with the Ressallah, which had not time to join at Seringapatam, 369 horses in the field This regiment had been employed on account of disturbances in the Lower Mahratta country at Davengherray, in the neighbourhood of Hurryhur On the 4th of July it only received the order to assemble for inspection at Coonghull, when at Chittledroog, and arrived only yesterday, having that day marched 28 miles No part of the regiment had marched less than 250 miles within the month, and a large part a great deal more

Their mares, however, were fat and in good condition Some of the men were taller than I had seen in the other corps I measured one 6 feet 2 inches, without his turban I saw a large portion previous to inspection in watering order, as I had done the other corps, and found them equally well mounted They had 60 carbines, all in a good serviceable state, as were their arms in general They expressed the same desire for their lancers to have a pistol, and some more carbines, as well as pouches for ammunition, besides the regiment to be allowed to breed from their mares The movements were very fairly performed, and their horses exceedingly well broke

"Having now made the inspection of five regiments of the Sillahdars, I am satisfied that they are a most serviceable kind of force, they can be assembled at any place with the greatest celerity, their knowledge of the country and its produce would be found of great service when moving as an auxiliary force with a regular army, and from the zeal they showed, and desire to serve, I feel confident that they may be relied on, and their fidelity insured, provided they continue to be regularly paid, and some little favours occasionally granted them —I have the honour to be, etc

"L LOVELL,
Brigr Inspecting Officer"

"KOLAR, *26th July* 1841

"*To* COLONEL M CUBBON, *Commissioner in Mysore*

"SIR,—In obedience to your orders, I made an inspection at this place of the Sixth Regiment of Sillahdar horse. They mustered in the field 352 horses

"They were all armed and clothed similarly to other corps I have already inspected, requiring some more carbines for the swordsmen, and pistols for the lancers, likewise pouches; the arms, although of very old pattern, did not any of them miss fire.

"I saw a great number of very superior mares, and their cattle were particularly well broke

"On the previous day, besides seeing part of them on foot and in watering order, a sham fight of outposts was performed, and I perceived they were quite *au fait* at that kind of desultory fighting, and seemed perfectly to understand the nature of skirmishing and ambuscades Their turban head-dress seems particularly well adapted to their service

"I find the words of command are given in Persian, they seem very long, and the Sillahdars have generally expressed a wish to have them given in English, as none or few of them understand Persian

"The same request was made as in the other corps regarding the breeding from their best mares

"I also beg to conclude in reporting that the whole arrangement of the corps does very great credit to Captain Macleod —I have the honour to be, etc

"L LOVELL,
Brigr Inspecting Officer

From MAJOR-GENERAL L LOVELL, K H, *Commanding Malabar and Canara, to* CAPTAIN MACLEOD, *Commanding the Sillahdar Horse of Mysore*

"SIR,—The services of the Sillahdar horse being no longer required upon this frontier, I now send them back to join their corps In doing so I beg leave to return my thanks for the service they have performed, being ready at all times for any duty required of them

"The Ressalah of horse under command of Ressaldar Mahomed Abas, and the Jemadar Goolam Hyder, who accompanied me to different posts, was always extremely well conducted

"I beg to recommend them to your notice, as well as to General Cubbon, Commissioner of Mysore, and trust the batta will be granted them the same as to the other troops employed on this frontier—I have the honour to be, etc etc

"L LOVELL,

Major-Gen Commanding Malabar and Canara

"SIRCEE, 31*st March* 1845"

I think that these Reports of General Lovell's, the testimonials of their conduct in the field, and my own Report, are sufficient to acquaint any one with the nature of the irregular forces of India, and of their importance as an auxiliary to our regular forces in times of war, and of their usefulness in time of peace. However, I trust the reader will pardon me in introducing the following testimonials, relative to the suppression of the insurrection at Canara, which will further illustrate the worth and use of the irregular forces of India when under the guidance of fit European officers. It will be seen from these testimonials that I made a Report on the causes and suppression of this insurrection, for which I received thanks from the Commissioner. I might here insert the whole of this Report, but I am of opinion that now it is not of that importance to the general reader as to justify its insertion The moral of the cause and suppression of the insurrection, however, is of the utmost moment as a maxim of government, and a great political truth, which of course is always of use to any government. The Canarese said to me that a country that paid our Government so well *ought to be protected;* that they had no nationality, and were merely determined in their loyalty by that government that would give them the best protection, that the rebels threatened to murder them and their families if they would not join them, at the same time saying that the English had not the power to protect them, that they were thus as it were forced to join them for their personal safety for the time being, from sheer want of protection, but that they had no desire to do so, and finally thanked me in having timely relieved them from the compulsion of the rebels, into those acts of violence which would have necessitated their punishment by the Government And I may venture to remark that India, from being one of the poorest and most unstable countries, may become one of the richest and happiest in the world, by being made perfectly safe; and I may add, that India will never be free, in the true sense of the term, until she is made perfectly safe, and this safety will most conveniently be effected by the Sillahdar system The following then are the testimonials which I and others received from the Commissioner of Mysore, from the Government of Madras, and from the Government of India on suppressing the Canara insurrection:—

Extract of a Letter to the SUPERINTENDENT OF NUGGUR, *dated* 16*th May* 1837

"It has been a gratifying duty to the Commissioner to bring to the notice of the Government of India the highly creditable conduct and useful services of both these officers,[1] as also the steadiness and perseverance, with the generally soldier-like behaviour displayed by the parties of Sowar and Barr employed under them respectively, and further to mark his own sense of the praiseworthy conduct of the latter, as well as in consideration of their services, having been employed in a foreign territory, the Commissioner authorizes a gratuity equal to two months' pay being presented to each of the native commissioned, non-commissioned, and privates of both establishments who were actually employed below the Ghauts To enable the Ilakee Cutcherees at the Huzoor to draw the amount, you will have the goodness to furnish nominal rolls of them at your earliest convenience The sums advanced by Captain Macleod will be deducted from the amount of gratuity now sanctioned, and be reimbursed to that officer (True Extract)

"A CLARKE, *Officiating Secretary*"

Extract of a Letter from the Chief Secretary to the Government of Fort St George to the Commissioner for the Government of the Territories of the Rajah of Mysore, dated 20*th May* 1837.

"The Right Honourable the Governor in Council has desired me to request that you will convey to the officers named in the margin[2] the thanks of this Government for the zeal and activity which they have respectively evinced

[1] Captain Macleod and the Honourable H B Devereux

[2] Mr H Stokes, Captain Lettardy, Captain F Hunter, Captain A Macleod, Mr Devereux, Lieutenant Montgomery

The rapid march of Captain Macleod on Mangalore, and the presence of Captain Hunter, Lieutenant Montgomery, and Mr Devereux on the confines of Canara, doubtless had the effect of preventing the extension of disaffection by giving confidence to the well-disposed inhabitants, and overawing those who might have entertained factious views.

(True Extract)

"A CLARKE, *Officiating Secretary.*"

No 390.

"*Mysore Commissioner's Office*

"*To* CAPTAIN MACLEOD, *Officiating Assistant to the Commissioner*

SIR,—I have the honour to transmit copy of a letter from Mr Secretary Macnaghton, under date the 5th ultimo, expressive of the high sense entertained by the Governor-General in Council of your valuable services on the occasion of the late rebellion in Canara, and to offer you my congratulations on this most honourable testimony of the approbation of the supreme authority in India —I have the honour to be, Sir, your most obedient servant,

"M CUBBON, *Commissioner*

"BANGALORE, 1st *July* 1837"

"*To* COLONEL M CUBBON, *Commissioner for the Government of the Territories of His Highness the Rajah of Mysore*

"*Police Department*—SIR,—I am now desired by the Right Honourable the Governor-General of India in Council to acknowledge receipt of your three letters of the dates and on the subjects noted in the margin.[1]

[1] Letter dated 12th May 1837 —Forwarding copy of a communication from the Superintendent of Nuggur, containing a report of the services

"2 The Governor-General in Council has much pleasure in recording his full concurrence in the praise which you have bestowed on the conduct of your assistants, Captains Hunter and Macleod, the Honourable Mr Devereux and Lieutenant Montgomery, on the occasion of the recent insurrection in Canara. The exertions of each of these gentlemen entitle him to the warmest thanks of Government, and you will be pleased to assure them that his Lordship in Council will not lose sight of the zeal and ability which they have severally displayed It was the good fortune of Captains Hunter and Macleod especially to have an opportunity of distinguishing themselves by the performance of enterprises of no ordinary gallantry, which were attended with eminent advantage to the interests of Government A general order to the above effect will shortly be promulgated for public information

"3 You have already been called upon to state what, in your opinion, would be a suitable reward for the fidelity and devotion displayed towards the British Government by the Coorg troops under the direction of the Dewan Bopoo during the recent insurrection, and you will now be pleased to report further as to the expediency or otherwise of signally noticing the good conduct of the Mysore troops on the same occasion.

"4 You have been apprised by my former communications

rendered by Captain Macleod and the Honourable Mr Devereux in preventing the spread of rebellion which lately prevailed in South Canara and noticing the good conduct of the Mysore troops

Do 13th May 1837 —Transmitting copy of a letter from the Superintendent of Coorg, with its enclosed correspondence with the principal collector of Canara, respecting the conduct of Dewan Bopoo and the body of Coorgs under his charge

Do 13th May 1837 —Transmitting copy of a letter, and of its enclosures, to the Chief Secretary to Government at Fort St George, on the subject of the disposal of the troops lately assembled for the purpose of acting against the rebels of Canara.

of the very high opinion which is entertained by Government of the merits and services of Captain Lettardy, Superintendent of Coorg, to whose conciliatory, firm, and judicious conduct the devotion to our cause displayed by the inhabitants of that district may chiefly be attributed.—I have, etc,

"W. H MACNAGHTON,

"*Secretary to Government of India*

"FORT WILLIAM, *5th June* 1837"

"(True Copy)

"A CLARKE, *Officiating Secretary*"

Extract of a Letter from Mr W H MACNAGHTEN, *dated Camp at Meerut the* 12*th February* 1838

"And his Lordship has been particularly gratified with the clear and concise statement furnished by Captain Macleod of his sentiments and proceedings in connexion with the late insurrection (True Extract)

"M. CUBBON"

"No. 782

"*Mysore Commissioner's Office*

"*To* CAPTAIN A. MACLEOD, *Officiating Assistant, Acting Superintendent Nuggur Division*

"SIR,—I have the honour to acquaint you that the Right Honourable the Governor-General of India has been pleased, under date 3d instant, to appoint you to be Military Assistant to the Commissioner for the affairs of Mysore in succession to Major Hunter, whose resignation has been accepted from the date of his embarkation for Europe.

"2. It gives me great satisfaction to annex for your information the following extract of a letter which I have received from the Private Secretary to the Governor-General:—

"'Lord Auckland has peculiar satisfaction in being able to reward the tried services of Captain Macleod by promoting him to be your Military Assistant[1] His Lordship instructs me to beg that you will communicate this paragraph of my letter to Captain Macleod.'

"3. You will of course continue in charge of the Nuggur Division until relieved by Lieutenant Halsted, who has been appointed Superintendent[2]—I have the honour to be, Sir, your most obedient servant,

"M. CUBBON, *Commissioner.*

"BANGALORE, 28*th December* 1838"

[1] Great was my reward for my bloodless exertions, but I made it my duty to do all I could to save and not to take life, and a kind Providence made my kind words, backed by fifty Sillahdars and an hundred Mysore regular infantry, successful

[2] I held charge of the division till December 1839. In six months Captain Halsted had caused so great disorder that I was sent out to relieve him. In five months more I handed the division over to the Honourable H B Devereux in as quiet and settled a state as it was when Captain Halsted received it in charge from me.

IV.

CONCLUSION.

THERE are many more truths referring to India that I would be most anxious to lay before the notice of the reader, but I must content myself, for various reasons, by concluding with a few desultory and unconnected remarks on one or two subjects of importance.

And first, let me say a few words more on the disbanded regiments of India. Just let me quote again the latter part of the 6th Madras Cavalry's Petition to the Queen:—

"May it please your Majesty therefore to hear our prayer It has become the source of great grief to us to have our hopes thus suddenly and entirely cut off, inasmuch as we are the sons of Sepoys who have had for generations, according to the custom of this country, no other way of living save that of being soldiers, and who, in this capacity, have so faithfully served the State for so many generations Up till this time, we confidingly believed that we in this regiment, and our offspring in future, would be treated in the same manner as our forefathers had been, while we faithfully continued to obey whatever orders we might receive, and serve wherever we might be required to go Since Mussulman kings have reigned in Hindostan, our race has always been faithfully employed as cavalry soldiers in their service; and, for the last century, since the British rule has existed, we have in the same capacity sacrificed our lives in defence of our flag We have no native country or home of our own; for the English camp has for generations been our birthplace, our only residence, and our home We are a race born faithfully to serve with our lives, and devote them for our sovereigns, but in consequence of the regiment's being disbanded, our hopes are suddenly cut off Consequently we are in a state of perplexity and dismay Moreover, from many causes, and from having made many long and arduous marches, we have become much reduced in circumstances and without pecuniary resources, so much so that we hardly dare venture to relate the same If it may please your Most Gracious Majesty to confer one favour on your ancient servants (namely, to re-embody our loyal and faithful regiment), your Majesty's humble petitioners will be able to pass their days in ease and happiness, and will for ever, while we continue to live, offer daily prayers for your Majesty's long life and prosperity."

What more could the most faithful army that ever served mankind say for their loyalty? Let not the fact of their petition having been written more than eleven years ago be any argument against a noble compliance with its prayer. True, eleven years look to be a long time, which assuredly it is in man's life; but the same period will appear trifling when compared with the loyal service of this very cavalry, as stated in their petition. That the Queen of Britain, after the lapse and silence of eleven years, should show that she has always the good of her subjects at heart, and that the Home Government should now comply with the request of their petition when a fit time occurred, would be strokes of political wisdom far superior to that which disbanded the regiments of the loyal Madras army, and would not only cancel and obliterate the past, but would cement between us and the natives of India a lasting friendship, and would certainly establish our dominion in the south of India against anything that might turn up.

And now let me tell in plain words the real native opinion of the disbanding of *the army that saved India.* They all consider it a breach of faith on the part of the British Government, and nothing short of re-embodying them will ever convince them of the good intentions of our Government towards the natives of India. They consider the simple act of disbanding as a breach of faith in itself. But over and above this, they look upon the whole course of policy that dictated this order as implying something more obnoxious than a breach of faith. I was repeatedly told that the "exigencies of the State" never necessitated the disbanding of any faithful regiment of India. The Madras cavalry bear implacable hatred to the descendants of Hyder Alli, because he caused the ruin of their chieftain, the Nabob of the Carnatic. After the 6th Light Cavalry was disbanded one of their great grievances was that at the very time "the exigencies of the State" caused their ruin, the same "State" increased the pensions of their enemies (Tippoo's sons).

But it is not only that Britain should not be chargeable with a breach of faith, but her policy should be truth even against outbursts of Indian perfidy. Lord Macaulay truly, wisely, and forcibly says —

"That 'Honesty is the best policy' is a maxim which we firmly believe to be generally correct, even with respect to the temporal interests of individuals, but with respect to societies, the rule is subject to still fewer exceptions, and that for this reason, that the life of societies is longer than the life of individuals It is possible to mention men who have owed great worldly prosperity to breaches of private faith But we doubt whether it be possible to mention a State which has on the whole been a gainer by a breach of public faith The entire history of British India is an illustration of the great truth that it is not prudent to oppose perfidy to perfidy, and that the most efficient weapon with which men can encounter falsehood is truth. During a long course of years, the English rulers of India, surrounded by allies and enemies whom no engagement could bind, have generally acted with sincerity and uprightness, and the event has proved that sincerity and uprightness are wisdom English valour and English intelligence have done less to extend and to preserve our Oriental Empire than English veracity All that we could have gained by imitating the doublings, the evasions, the fictions, the perjuries which have been employed against us, is as nothing when compared with what we have gained by being the one power in India on whose word reliance can be placed No oath which superstition can devise, no hostage however precious, inspires a hundredth part of the confidence which is produced by the 'yea, yea,' and 'nay, nay,' of a British envoy. No fastness, however strong by art or nature, gives to its inmates a security like that enjoyed by the chief who, passing the territories of powerful and deadly enemies, is armed with the British guarantee The mightiest princes of the East can scarcely, by the offer of enormous usury, draw forth any portion of the wealth which is concealed under the hearths of their subjects The British Government offers little more than four per cent, and avarice hastens to bring forth ten millions of rupees from its most secret repositories A hostile monarch may promise mountains of gold to our Sepoys, on condition that they will desert the standard of the Company The Company only promises a moderate pension after a long service But every Sepoy knows that the promise of the Company will be kept, he knows that if he lives a hundred years his rice and salt are as secure as the salary of the Governor-General, and he knows that there is not another State in India which would not, in spite of the most solemn vows, leave him to die of hunger in a ditch as soon as he had ceased to be useful The greatest advantage which a government can possess is to be the one trustworthy government in the midst of governments which nobody can trust"

May this ever be the character of our Government, as it truly has been its character hitherto Only I think there have been exceptional deviations from this truly noble characteristic, arising from mistaken notions of political government, and truly if ever there was an opportunity afforded to the natives of India of upbraiding Britain for want of faith, it is furnished in this the disbanding of the loyal Madras regiments.

It is not possible for me to predict what our

Government may think proper to do or undo on this momentous question; but I can console myself with the conviction that an ever-watchful Providence has enabled me to do my duty in laying the whole matter plainly before the Government, the people of England and of India; and, moreover, that I have thus fought the best battle I could fight for *the army that saved India*, if not for the safety and well-being of both England and India. I would ask the most unbelieving in the good faith of natives of India, what would England's position in India now be had the Madras and Bombay Sepoys acted towards their European officers as did the Bengal Sepoys in the great mutiny?

I may here mention that the Madras cavalry, ever since taken under our own Government, has ever had in its ranks a sufficient complement of Hindoo officers, rank and file, to relieve all Mahometans of taking any duty whatever in hand during the time of a Mahometan feast The two castes amalgamated like brothers. Nor were the *Christian* trumpeters and farriers of the 6th Cavalry other than on the same terms with their brother troopers. Indeed, I have never seen but brotherly love throughout the native Madras cavalry, whether they were Hindoos, Mahometans, or Christians. This mixture of castes has many advantages. Our great enemy, Mahomed Alli of Mysore, prided himself on his freedom from all caste prejudices And some of his fine aged Maho metan officers, who, above thirty years ago, served under me in Mysore, never hesitated to allow that that conqueror's best infantry were Roman Catholic Christians. And I might have stated earlier that at one time during the mutiny the Mahometan commander of the Mysore infantry furnished the Commissioner's and my own house-guards out of the descendants of these very Christians who were converted to Christianity by Portuguese priests at a very early period The great body, however, of the Madras cavalry consists of Mahometan Sepoys whose ancestors emigrated from Arabia into India under their chieftain at a very remote period of history. If the good fortune were to happen to them to be restored to serve as Sillahdars, they would have the most glorious prestige of any troops in the world It may be nothing short of truth to assume that after a glorious and ever loyal and victorious service of a thousand years, they would be restored to what their forefathers originally were, namely, peaceable breeders of horses, and possibly (as they now in the capacity of Sillahdars would be) keepers and preservers of the public peace, and the security against robbers of personal property, or against invasion, in the event of any attack such as our periodicals make some of us fear and believe to be possible, if not probable, in the present uncertain state of native feeling with respect to our present position in India

Before dropping this subject, let me insert what

ended my official correspondence as commanding officer at the head of my regiment, which will serve to show the type of the character of the men that were disbanded, and also show to what source their sterling character owed its origin :—

From the OFFICER COMMANDING THE 6TH LIGHT CAVALRY *to the* ADJUTANT-GENERAL OF THE ARMY

"No 399 "BANGALORE, 31*st December* 1860

"SIR,—I have the honour to inform you that I was this morning waited upon by Jemadar Adjutant Shaik Emom, of the 6th Regiment Light Cavalry, with a document of which a copy is inserted in the margin, and as it appears to me to be probable that his Excellency the Commander-in-chief might not wish so distinguished a native officer to lose the pay of his staff appointment, I trust to be pardoned for soliciting that you will kindly submit his case to his Excellency Sir Patrick Grant, K C B

"A MACLEOD, *Colonel*"

"Jemadar Shaik Emom served in my troop when the regiment was on field-service in Bengal during the mutiny, and his conduct both in camp and in action was deserving of the warmest praise On one occasion, when under a hot fire from the enemy, I was forming my troop for a charge, he galloped up from the rear (his proper station, and where he was comparatively protected) and placed himself between my person and the enemy, saying, 'They will all take aim at you, as you are a European, but they will not care so much for me'

"G H M AYNSLEY, *Captain, in Charge of E Troop*"

The following was the result of my recommendation —

"Military Department.

"Proceedings of Madras Government.

"Memorandum from the Adjutant-General of the Army, Fort St. George, 8th January 1861, No 14 —'In forwarding the accompanying letter from the officer commanding 6th Regiment Light Cavalry, dated 31st December 1860, No. 399, the Commander-in-chief has the honour to recommend that, in consideration of the gallant conduct in the field of Jemadar Adjutant Shaik Emom, of the above corps, the staff allowance of his appointment may be continued to him until he can be absorbed, on the occurrence of a vacancy, in the appointment of Jemadar Adjutant in the regiment to which he has been transferred 2 Had the Jemadar's gallant conduct been brought to notice at the time of its occurrence, Lieutenant-General Sir Patrick Grant would probably have proposed that a step of rank should have been conferred on him'"

"*Order No* 205, 17*th January* 1861

"Sanctioned as recommended."

From the Officer Commanding 6th Regiment Light Cavalry *to the* Adjutant-General of the Army

"Sir,—With reference to G O C C, dated 22d December 1860, I have the honour to report, for the information of his Excellency the Commander-in-chief, that, as far as practicable, the orders under that head have been carried out[1]

"I trust to be permitted on such an occasion as this, to submit to his Excellency my conviction, as an old Madras cavalry officer, that faithfully and admirably though the

[1] *i.e.* disbanding the Regiment

Sepoys of the 6th Light Cavalry undoubtedly behaved during the mutinies, their conduct depended upon, and was in the hands of, their European officers Kind and considerate to all ranks, the officers with the regiment had the affections of all to an extent of which I can best convey an idea by giving in English what one of their best native officers lately told me He said, 'The European officers of our regiment were so good that any Sepoy would have placed his body between such gentlemen and the bullets of the enemy' Of the truth of that statement I have not a doubt, and the officers who were with the regiment in Bengal far from doubt it, and none knew better than they the stamp of men they had to depend upon, but it was the kindness and consideration of these officers to all under them that made the Sepoys so devoted to them And what more can any Government wish for in soldiers than that they so love and think of their officers as to feel that their lives on service are more valuable than their own?[1]

"A MACLEOD, *Colonel*,

Commanding late 6th Regiment Light Cavalry

"BANGALORE, 31*st January* 1861"

[1] That our Indian fellow-subjects are susceptible of entertaining false impressions beyond an Englishman's suspicions, is surely clearly shown in what has been told of the greased cartridges To many also what has, since Lord William Bentinck was Governor-General, been known throughout the Madras army as the *Batta Order*, will appear equally incomprehensible The fact must first be told that in the year 1809 the European officers of the Madras army and the Government had an alarming difference, which almost broke out into open mutiny The Sepoys stood by their officers to a man, and at that time, and for many years after, wherever and whenever officers of a regiment were on full *batta*, it was the same with the men, until about 1834 an order came through the Bengal Government which authorized full batta to all officers serving with regiments at stations above 200 miles from their Presidency But the natives were to be on half batta. It soon became known to intelligent European officers that their Sepoys looked upon the order, on the part of Government, as a trick, with the intention of what they called putting the men in different boats from their officers, in the hope the Sepoys would not stand

From the ADJUTANT-GENERAL OF THE ARMY *to* COLONEL MACLEOD, *Commanding late 6th Regiment Light Cavalry*

"SIR,—I have the honour, by the order of the Commander-in-chief, to acknowledge the receipt of your letter of the 31st ultimo, reporting that the orders in G O C C, 22d December 1860, have been carried out as far as practicable, and bringing to notice the feeling existing between the officers and men of that regiment 2 It gives the Commander-in-chief the greatest pleasure to receive this testimony to the excellent feeling which has bound together in one common bond of attachment the European and native ranks of the 6th Light Cavalry. It is alike highly creditable to both parties, and most conducive to the interests of the public service

W G WOODS, *Lieutenant-Colonel,*
Adjutant-General of the Army

"ADJUTANT GENERAL'S OFFICE,
FORT ST GEORGE, *6th February* 1861"

At Bangalore a Mahometan Subadar of my late regiment said to me in Hindustani, in great anger, that it was very shameful to disband a regiment whose European officers so regularly attended church. This the officers truly did, in accordance with General Sir Augustus Spenser's official request. I attribute the fact that all, men and officers, did their utmost to obtain the good opinion of General

true to their officers when without the full batta which their officers enjoyed I was often assured by natives that Madras Sepoys were too loyal seriously to have any real wish to mutiny, but why they so often made trouble about batta, was in the hope Government would give in, and make them happy in the same boat with their officers, as were their fathers and grandfathers. I give this as a truth, of which Government can find proof by sending for and questioning old Madras officers, either in England or India.

Sir Augustus Spenser (now Commander-in-chief of the army of Bombay), entirely to their knowledge that he was a just man, whose good opinion would reflect credit upon every man in the regiment, from the commanding officer through every rank, even to the very horse-keeper. But this remark of the Mahometan's shows also what I have always found to be the case, namely, that the natives of India pay particular respect to those Europeans who are as observant of their religion as they themselves are of theirs. I attribute my success in managing the natives on every occasion, not only to keeping good faith with them, but also to my befriending such as were religious in matters of caste Preserving caste by a native of India is the same as preserving position by a European gentleman. We blame them for want of truth, but may this not arise from the fact that they have been so long a conquered race? Yet it is a strange fact, however little they are affected by the non-observance of truth themselves, they almost worship those who are strict observers of the truth, and in whom they can place implicit confidence. In both my civil and military capacities in India I succeeded with natives, as they had all the confidence of a brother in me. Without any education but a perfect knowledge of native character, I managed the Nuggur Division, where a gentleman of the highest culture and intelligence failed from sheer ignorance of native character, and for which I received the following testimonial.—

"No 686

"*Mysore Commissioner's Office*

"*To* CAPTAIN MACLEOD, *Military Assistant*

"SIR,—Adverting to your letter of the 5th instant, No 369, reporting that you had delivered over charge of the Nuggur Division to the Honourable H B Devereux, I have the honour, by desire of the Commissioner, to convey to you his best thanks for the attention you gave to the Civil duties of that Division, in addition to those of your own office, while you were in charge of it —I have the honour to be, etc etc, A CLARKE, *Offg Secretary*

"BANGALORE, 19*th November* 1840"

"True Copy."

NOTE.—The truth is, the natives did the work for me, and I had such power over them that they did *all* the work for me, both civil and military A MACLEOD

It may appear not to be altogether consistent with taste to say so much where I myself am so much concerned, and to insert these testimonials, but my main object is to show upon what basis we can firmly build in the heart of the native of India, and to show how easily he is governed and kept loyal. And if the native of India has many weak points of character, there is one thing in which he sets us, and I believe all other nations, a bright example. His sobriety and temperance are truly astonishing, and are not only worthy of commendation, but of imitation.

If we could only trust the natives of India, and place implicit faith in their loyalty, and show them in action as well as word that we wish to do to them as we would that they should do unto us, they are the first men in the world to appreciate our candour and Christian spirit, and the last to abuse our confidence or forsake us in the hour of need.

My service in India exceeded thirty-nine years; and my actual performance of duty exceeded thirty-six years. All the leave I have ever had, put together, was no more than two years ten months and sixteen days. I am now an old man; and all my life I have studied men, and not books. No man had ever better opportunities to benefit by such a turn of mind. It was simply becoming a native myself, as it were, among them, that on all occasions they were more than willing to obey me, and that I got what was most hidden in the native mind with regard to the past and future of India, and which I now offer to the public, in the firm belief that I am led to do so by a guiding hand, not only to avert disaster and calamity, but to effect great and positive good, by impartially holding up the glass to both Europeans and Indians, that they may be enabled, not only to see each other, but themselves, which may help to engender those mutual feelings of toleration and charity which cement nations as well as families, and at the same time to dispel all those feelings of mistrust that breed contention and war, and eventually lead to ruin, by making both an easy prey to the foreign aggressor, who will entail upon the one national humiliation, and upon the other centuries of subjugation and consequent retrogression into the sloughs of degradation and barbarism, from which they have been slowly but gradually emerging for the last century.

I have said already that it would be well that our Government should afresh issue Her Majesty's proclamation referring to India. The enlightened reader may have discovered in reading this book that my aim ever was to convince the natives of India under me that it was an utter impossibility for any man by any means to convert them to Christianity against their own will; and I believe that such a re-issue at the present time would have the effect of deepening and confirming that conviction. Since the foregoing was printed it has been my good fortune to get the Calcutta newspaper called *The Friend of India*, of April 12, 1872, from which the following is reprinted, being the speech of our present Governor-General of India, without remark, and with which I end my book. On March 9th Lord Northbrook dined with the Mayor of Winchester, and made a very good speech. He said —

"I feel all the stronger from the great success of him who has gone before me in filling that office All I can say on that subject is, that I do feel my deficiency, and it is only by the blessing of God and by the exercise of all the energies in my power, that I can hope in any way to fulfil its duties. . . . It would be rash, indeed, in me to express any opinions at the present time with the imperfect knowledge I can only have as yet. A subject of Her Majesty who goes to share in the administration of India has one great advantage in this—he has no new policy to propound. The great principles of Indian administration have been placed on record in a document which will form one of the leading landmarks in the history of India. I refer to the proclamation which was issued by Her Majesty at the time when the wisdom of Parliament substituted the direct government of the Crown for that of the magnificent Company which had governed for many generations, with, as I believe, wisdom and success, our Eastern empire In that proclamation the great principles of Indian policy have been enunciated; and on this occasion it may not be improper, if you will allow me, to read one or two passages as indicating the main principles—for it is well we should look back to some of the first principles—of our Indian administration The Queen says —'*We desire no extension of our present territorial possessions; and, while we will permit no aggression upon our dominions or our rights to be attempted with impunity, we shall sanction no encroachment on those of others. We shall respect the rights, dignity, and honour of native princes as our own, and we desire that they as well as our own subjects should enjoy that prosperity and that social advancement which can only be secured by internal peace and good government. We hold ourselves bound to the natives of Indian territories by the same obligations of duty which bind us to all other subjects, and those obligations, by the blessing of Almighty God, we shall faithfully and conscientiously fulfil. Firmly relying ourselves on the truth of Christianity, and acknowledging with gratitude the solace of religion, we disclaim alike the right and the desire to impose our convictions on any of our subjects. We declare it to be our royal will and pleasure that none be in any wise favoured, none molested or disquieted by reason of their religious faith or observances, but that all shall alike enjoy the equal and impartial protection of the law; and we do strictly charge and enjoin all those who may be in authority under us, that they abstain from all interference with the religious belief or worship of any of our subjects, on pain of our highest displeasure. And it is our further will, that so far as may be, our subjects, of whatever race or creed, be freely and impartially admitted to offices in our service, the duties of which they may be qualified by their education, ability, and integrity duly to discharge. We know and respect the feelings of attachment with which the natives of India regard the lands inherited by them from their ancestors, and we desire to protect them in all rights connected therewith, subject to the equitable demands of the State; and we will that generally in framing and administering the law due regard be paid to the ancient rights, usages, and customs of India.'* A servant of the Crown who goes to India to take part in its administration will not, in my opinion, fail to perform his duty, if he should carry out these principles as stated in Her Majesty's proclamation. The difference between Eastern and Western civilisation, and the danger of being carried away by the ideas of what may be right and politic and wise in this country, when we come to deal with a different country—a people with different sentiments, different religions, different education, and a different tone of thought from ourselves. That lesson, at any rate, I hope to carry with me to India. Difficult indeed would be the task of any one who leaves the shores of England to occupy a post of great responsibility in the far East if he had not the assistance of able administrators having a full knowledge of the feelings and interests of the people with whom they are brought into contact. But the servants of the Crown who go to India have this peculiar advantage—they have, to assist them, that magnificent service, the civil and military service of India—a service which has been justly pronounced second to none in the world—men who, when placed in a position of difficulty and danger, have always proved themselves equal to any occasion,—and who have been actuated during the whole of their career with one desire only—the welfare of the people of India over whom they have to exercise authority."

The greatness of the ideas of Her Majesty's proclamation fill my mind with the conviction that Her Majesty and our Government, by carrying out the prayer of the petition of the 6th Light Cavalry to the extent of re-embodying as Sillahdars the four disbanded regiments, will, by such a truly Christian act, cause natives themselves to enter voluntarily into the very spirit of Christianity.

EDINBURGH: T. AND A. CONSTABLE,
PRINTERS TO THE QUEEN, AND TO THE UNIVERSITY.